D1147275

Lets
Work

PETER LANG is a freelance writer, environmental consultant and events organiser. He is a member of the national LetsLink speakers panel which gives talks and advice to groups starting and running Lets schemes. He is a co-founder of his local Malvern Lets and has assisted networks in the Welsh Borders and English home counties.

He is the co-ordinator of Green & Away which organises the national Lets Camp, the largest gathering of Lets members in the UK. Green & Away arranges environmental camps, conferences and meetings for a wide range of groups.

Peter Lang has been a writer for over 20 years and has contributed to a wide range of newspapers, magazines and radio stations. He has also worked for many campaigning organisations and local authorities.

He was a partner in The Environmental Surveys Company, an environmental consultancy. He is a member of the UK Green Party and has worked as their national press officer.

Lets Work

Rebuilding the local economy

Peter Lang

Illustrated by
Robert Richards

GROVER
BOOKS

First published 1994 by Grover Books.

Grover Books is an imprint of Worldly Goods.

Worldly Goods distributes books on ecology, the environment, society and agriculture. For further details write to Worldy Goods, 10–12 Picton Street, Montpelier, Bristol BS6 5QA.

Text © Peter Lang. The right of Peter Lang to be identified as the author of this work has been asserted in accordance with the Copyright, Designs and Patents Act 1988.

Copyright in the photographs is held by the photographers. Copyright in the illustrations is held by Robert Richards.

All rights reserved. No part of this book may be reproduced, stored in a retrieval system or transmitted in any form or by any means electronic, photocopying, recording or otherwise without the prior permission in writing of the publisher.

ISBN 1 899233 00 8

Designed and typset by Sarah Tyzack, Oxford.
Cover design by Helen Miller.

Printed and bound by Biddles Ltd., Guildford and King's Lynn.

To Clara May

When money is the basis of life,
joy will sit with a drooping head.
PHILIP OYLER,
THE GENEROUS EARTH, 1950

Contents

Preface

In the mid 1980s Local Exchange Trading Systems (Lets) were barely known in the UK. People exchanged goods and services by cash, cheque or credit card, or did each other small occasional favours across the garden fence.

Since then Lets has come of age and at the time of writing (May 1994) new systems were being formed in the UK at the rate of more than one a week. A similar picture is emerging in other countries. People are enthusiastically discovering the value of exchanging goods and services without using the money issued by governments.

They do so because it means the money they have goes further, and because, once in Lets, they see it is a way of meeting new friends in their town or city, as well as being a very effective way of regenerating the local economy. Lets values people's skills and allows them to use them freely in their local community.

Unlike so many business or community initiatives, Lets does not need council permission, government grants or bank loans to start. Nor is any special knowledge needed. A small group of people can have a system up and running in a few weeks.

All they need to do to launch a system is create their Lets units. They do this by giving them a name and a rough value. They then offer goods and services to each other by listing them in a directory. To trade, members simply contact each other, agree a price expressed in the Lets units, and commission the job. Then the transaction is recorded on the Lets accounts by a member who acts as a book keeper. Unlike national currencies, the members don't need to be in possession of Lets before they spend them: they create them by agreeing to go into debit, thereby making a commitment to the other members to do some work in return later on.

Imagine you are a member of a Lets group and you discover a burst pipe. You look in the Lets directory and phone a fellow member who offers plumbing. When the job is done you pay using a Lets cheque at the price in Lets you have both agreed. The plumber sends the Lets cheque to the administrator who debits your account and credits the plumber's. You've entered into a commitment to do some work on Lets in the future, and when the accounts are published the other members will know of your commitment and the credit to the plumber.

Yet despite the popularity of Lets here and abroad, this is the first time a complete guide to setting up and running a system has been published in book form both for readers who are new to Lets and for experienced administrators and traders. The book includes useful ideas to stimulate trading, and shows how Lets is being used and adapted by many different communities.

Lets is still very new, and some of the questions asked, particularly the legal queries, cannot always be answered clearly. Operating and trading on Lets is fully within the law, but it is unclear whether the courts will view Lets credits as money or barter. This discussion is likely to run and run, and the outcome will affect how Lets is treated by many regulatory agencies.

Similarly there are no clear answers as to how the systems will evolve as members come up with new ideas to adapt them. One such idea involves running an account heavily in debit to pay the extra costs of trading incurred by people with disabilities, say, or the parents of small children.

The only experience we have to draw on to gain an insight into issues such as these is how people behave when spending their national currency. But such comparisons are only of limited use when considering Lets, for Lets units are very different from conventional money. We are seeing that people behave very differently when trading in Lets.

Much of the trading in national currencies is based on grabbing the best financial opportunity with little thought for the effects on people or the environment. But trading in Lets brings out other considerations as people get to know their neighbours and their needs and wants. Such knowledge and contact is restoring the sense of community so lacking in today's industrialised world. In particular, it is bringing back that sense of community with the people we trade with: no longer are we mainly confined to buying and selling from faceless individuals or companies.

The 1990s are seeing the first regular use of a system of exchange where people create the unit of measure themselves as they need it. Lets are open to all to join and use. Their benefits and potential are clear. And if you don't yet have a system in your area, one can be started with only a little work...

Lets Work was written in response to the questions people new to Lets are asking. It sets out to describe how systems in the UK are trading and how they have evolved. It is intended as a guide for people who have heard of Lets and want to know in more detail how to participate. It is also the first attempt to document and celebrate the diversity of systems in a book. It examines the various structures which have evolved since Michael Linton, now working through the company Landsman, first coined the term in 1983.

Many UK groups, while acknowledging that their structure has evolved away from Landsman's definition, point to the success of Lets in this country, an achievement that stands in its own right. The word Lets has been used in the book to describe the generality of these structures, and to explain their diversity.

I hope the book achieves its aim of helping readers understand how Lets works, and how they can benefit from using their local system.

Your own local system may arrive at different answers to many of the questions the book raises. That is the joy of Lets; the systems are local for people in a community to use as they wish, to learn from as they wish, and to benefit from as they wish.

Acknowledgements

Thanks are due to many people whose dedication to Lets assisted with the production of this book.

Firstly to Val Oldaker who first introduced me to Lets — and convincingly answered my sceptical questioning about why people didn't just run up huge debts and run off; to Clara Slater for persuading me that writing the book would be both useful and enjoyable, and who read all the manuscripts with a practised eye; and to Jon Carpenter who edited the text and gave valued support throughout.

Thanks also are due to Sandra Bruce, Richard Knights,

Siobhan Harpur, Keith Mitchell, Jo Bend, Kos Kossowski, Peter Gay, Ruth Zimmerman, Andrew Grant, Chris Martley, Andy Rickford, David Wardle, Nigel Leach, John and Mandy Winkworth, Mick Coles, Maggie Mills, Ken Palmerton, Jane Hera, Niki Kortvellyessy, Jackie Kreel of NACAB and the many representatives of local and central government departments who answered my many obscure queries.

Finally Lets has benefited greatly from the work of its inventor Michael Linton, and from the work of Liz Shephard, Harry Turner and Daniel Johnson at LetsLink UK.

Peter Lang
May 1994

CHAPTER I

Money: what it is and how it lets us down

There is 90 times more money in the world than goods and services.

THE WORLD BANK

M y family were steeped in the world of commerce and shopkeeping: my father and aunts and uncles ran shops in London's East End. My father's view of money has always been that it is a record of work done: we do some work, we get some money, and that's a record of the time the work took, and the skill and experience it needed.

In fact, this is a good description of Local Exchange Trading Systems: they are a method of keeping a record of work done. If national money fulfilled only this function there would be less need for Lets.

In the days before banking and other financial services became so dominant in our society, most money was used as a measure of work done or goods exchanged. But nowadays large sums money are made (and lost) in our complex society without any work being done or any goods exchanged. Millions are won and lost on stock exchanges as the markets rise and fall according to confidence that things are going well or not so well. Huge amounts of cash can be picked up by speculators exchanging one currency for another. And banks earn large sums as they charge us interest on loans.

All these are examples of money being 'earned' where work is not done, because someone somewhere has money to spare which is not needed for living and can therefore be invested.

At the same time there is much work in our world needing to be done, many people willing and able to do it, but seemingly insufficient money to pay them.

Governments and money

Money evolved in order that people could exchange goods and services. Yet in the closing years of the twentieth century when using and regulating money is a fine art, there appears to be insufficient money available to do the very things it was invented for in the first place.

The government, which regulates the amount of money in the economy, attempts to keep the economy healthy by adjusting the amount of cash printed and using such tools as interest rates.

It does so with the aim of 'bearing down on inflation' and increasing the Gross National Product. It uses money to measure the state of the economy but there is little corresponding consideration of people's willingness to work. And as it controls the economy it has many conflicting desires: it wants to encourage

businesses to grow — but also wants to keep down inflation. It wants to 'get people back to work' — but also wants a 'competitive' labour market. It wants fewer people unemployed so there is less drain on the social security budget — but it also wants industry to increase output per worker, which results in fewer people being employed. It wants to encourage investors abroad to put their cash into Great Britain PLC, but also wants profits to accrue to people in Britain so the money is returned to the British economy.

So what is the lesson to be learnt from this? Money (in the form of national currencies) is trying to do too many things for too many people. It has become a commodity in itself so large sums of money can be earned from trading in money, instead of investing it with individuals and companies which can use it to undertake the activities we need to survive. The results are economies which boom and bust coupled with a serious lack of cash for everyday trading in the goods and services which we all need. What follows, as we all know, is economic recession with those still in work worried how long it will last, and those out of it living in a world of hopelessness and poverty.

So what is this beast that has grown out of the cowrie shells and gold coins which were the first currencies? What is money if it is not a record of work done? In the past, cash in the form of banknotes was simply paper representing gold which the government kept stashed in bank vaults. In 1844 the wording on the notes 'I promise to pay the bearer the sum of...' meant that the government would give a customer notes and coin of the realm to the face value of £3 17s 10d for every ounce of gold brought in — and vice versa.

Crisis and confidence

Nowadays, as Britain is no longer on the Gold Standard, notes cannot be exchanged for gold 'on demand' and *the cash itself has become the wealth*, even though a banknote is merely a piece of paper. It only represents wealth because we all believe it is wealth, that is, *we have confidence in it*.

I know that if you give me a pound coin or a dollar bill, the woman in the market will accept it for my weekly groceries. She knows her landlord will accept it towards the rent. He knows he can use it at the butcher's shop ... and so on.

The problem is that the value of the money I'm expecting from you is affected by all the other uses that money is put to — the stock exchange, the futures market, gilts and bonds, currency exchanges and so on. Indeed its very existence is decided upon by finance ministers with the thoughts of the financial markets uppermost in their mind, and the needs of you and me somewhat lower down their list of priorities.

The greatest irony is that an item introduced to allow people to trade with each other is now actively preventing that trading because it's in short supply where it's needed.

THE ABSURDITY OF IT

Ross Dobson writing in *Bringing the Economy Home from the Market* quotes the sixties writer Alan Watts as saying the Great Depression of the 1930s 'was not so much tragic as absurd'. He points out that 'all the same materials, all the same factories, all the same farms, all the same people, all the same skills, were all still available and all still in place. There were stockpiles of food and goods and raw materials available. But the economy was paralysed because there was no money. To say that people cannot exchange value with one another because there is no money is like saying you cannot build a house because you have no feet and inches.'

The return to community

Another major drawback of money is that it makes no contribution to building and strengthening people's sense of belonging to communities. This is a subject few economists will consider, but because money can flow anywhere at any time, most people barely consider where they are sending it. Some might claim that money doesn't exist to encourage people to feel they belong to a community — it simply exists as a medium of exchange.

But after our needs for food, clothing and shelter are met, a crying need for many of us is to feel we belong: to feel at ease where we live and comfortable with our fellow citizens.

Money does nothing to contribute to this feeling, and as the global market permeates even more of our lives, so our use of money involves more anonymous people in anonymous places. Indeed in competitive economies money can contribute to the breakup of communities.

Apart from the lack of emotions and feelings in the global market place, there are sound environmental reasons for us to 'shop local'. The more our money goes to people and institutions far away, the higher the environmental cost of bringing the goods to us. Bringing apples from New Zealand and cars from Japan is wreaking havoc with our environment as lorries plough through our cities and countryside exhaling gases which harm both the upper and lower levels of the atmosphere we rely on for our survival. Money spent far away assists multinational companies to find the cheapest labour market, whereas *money created and spent locally* will be spent locally again, and again, and again.

So if money could be used to encourage people to identify with their community, there would be an added advantage to it: it would give social as well as economic benefits.

These then are the drawbacks of conventional money: the amount of it available is controlled by the government, the use of it for non-productive activities means there is insufficient available for us to trade what we all need, and it helps to alienate people from their communities.

What we need is a substitute for national money or at least a system that works in parallel to it, which doesn't have these drawbacks and which actually contributes to a better life for us.

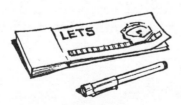

CHAPTER 2

How Lets works

*'There are so many people with
things to offer that are really
wanted by other people, but the
money in between is lacking.
Someone needs to create the
money.'*
Maggie Mills

The great attraction of Local Exchange Trading Systems is that any group of people can start them without waiting for grant money, premises, permission or expert community development skills. You — literally — just do it. In as little as four weeks individuals without any special skills can get together and have Lets up and trading.

Lets circumvents the drawbacks of national money by allowing people to build their own local economy using their own local units.

While sterling is *national*, Lets is *local*. It is used by an association of people in a village, town, or city district to trade among themselves.

Where Lets originated

Although local money can be found in history, the advent of state banking caused it to fall into disuse. However in the 1970s there were a number of experiments in sophisticated barter schemes in both the UK and the USA. These used time as the basis of the currency, or even the value of a basket of locally made goods.

However the LETSystem was designed by Michael Linton as a response to high unemployment in his home town in Comox Valley, British Columbia in Canada. The concept that people could create their own money evolved as the first personal computers appeared, making it easier for voluntary groups to record the large numbers of transactions without (illegally) issuing banknotes or coins. Lets in Britain grew after Michael Linton introduced his LETSystem and David Weston advocated a similar 'Community Exchange' scheme.

Michael Linton defines a LETSystem by five criteria:

- it is non-profit making,
- there is no compulsion to trade,
- information about balances is available to all members,
- the Lets unit is equal in value to the national currency,
- no interest is charged or paid.

The designer of the LETSystem maintains these criteria are not negotiable and in this book the term LETSystem is used to describe only Lets which meet all these criteria, which are more fully described in the Appendix.

In the years since 1983 thousands of people around the world have adapted these ideas in a variety of ways and use the word Lets to describe their systems. As far as is known, however, all are non-profit making, are not charging interest, will disclose members' balances, and rely on members creating the money by entering into trade. Many do not match their Lets unit to the national currency, however, and this issue is dealt with more fully in Chapter 12.

What Lets is

The participants form an association and create a unit of exchange and offer goods and services to each other priced in these units. The offers and wants are listed in a directory and individuals set their own rates and decide both who they want to trade with and how much trading they want to do. The association keeps a record of the transactions by means of cheques written in the local Lets units. These cheques are filed with a treasurer who in effect works as a bank by sending out regular statements of account to the members. The difference between the Lets accounts and a conventional bank is that no actual cash is issued (all transactions are by cheque) and no interest is charged or paid out.

JUST DO IT!

While helping your community can be fulfilling for many people, for others it can resemble a treadmill. A community group campaigning for change can spend hours writing letters and posting leaflets through doors. Parents trying to persuade a council to put a pedestrian crossing outside a school will need to do much work arranging meetings with councillors to make their case. It's no wonder most people are barely involved in their local community life.

But Lets is different. You just get together a few friends and start!

That is the greatest joy of Lets. It allows in a breath of fresh air to the work of community regeneration.

At its simplest you could be trading immediately a dozen people have gathered in your front room and they've got their minds around how it works.

So ... just do it!

Creating the Lets units

The individual members of the association decide how many Lets units are to be in circulation by the actual trading they do, and anyone can join.

Unlike the world of national currencies — and this is crucial — members don't need to be in possession of Lets before spending them.

When members create Lets units by *spending* when they have not yet *earned*, they are committing themselves to doing some work on the system at some time in the future. In Lets jargon, many people describe this as 'being in commitment'. They are *not going into debt* as they would if they had borrowed money from a high street bank. And while they are waiting for opportunities to meet this commitment, no interest is being charged on their minus balance. In the words of Daniel Johnson of LetsLink, the UK national Lets development agency, being in debt on Lets is 'a social service' because it allows others to spend and accrue wealth.

It follows therefore that the number of Lets units in existence exactly matches the amount of real wealth being exchanged. When the minus balances and the plus balances of the members are added up — they come to zero. There's nothing there really — but lots of trading has been done.

Generally systems place no limit on the amount members go into minus balance or 'commitment'. They can place a limit if they think it wise to do so, and they can assist members to obtain work to reduce minus balances by, for example, signalling in the directory that the person is particularly eager to trade, or drawing out skills or services they can offer.

The work involved in maintaining the Lets accounts and producing the directory is funded by taking a small Lets commission from each member which is paid to the people who do these jobs.

NAMING THE LETS UNIT

Members starting Lets networks have the opportunity to exercise their creativity when naming their Lets units. In Manchester they're called Bobbins because the city was built on the cotton industry. In Newbury they call them New Berries. Totnes has Acorns because from small acorns mighty oaks do grow... Malvern uses Beacons because of the beacons which used to shine out from the tops of the Malvern Hills.

In Bishops Castle on the Welsh Marches they trade in Offas after Offa's Dyke. And in St Leonards on the South Coast transactions are carried out in Gems. In Kent (nearer to mainland Europe than most of us) some wag suggested the ECU — which obviously stands for the East

Kent Unit (notwithstanding the difference between a 'C' and a 'K'). In Canada and Australia many systems simply call their Lets units 'green dollars'.

But think of the impression your name is going to give to the public before choosing one. In York, trade is done in Yorkies. But would the inhabitants of Goole be happy to trade in Goolies? And what would people in Bristol think of exchanging Bristols?

The ethics of Lets

Lets is a community resource, it is not a design for a private business, and not only is there no need for a system to be 'owned' by an individual or company, it is unlikely to work effectively if it is.

The system is strictly non-profit making and its activities are solely those the members as a whole agree to. There is no opportunity for speculating or earning interest in Lets, and people's trading balances are open for inspection by any member — a considerable difference from the world of banking.

Unlike conventional banking, the administrators of the accounts only transfer Lets credits as instructed by the members, and the various administrative charges are set by the members as a whole.

This is especially important both morally and because Lets works by building up trust between members, and they need to feel it is their system — they are not just customers of a bank or shop.

At the time of writing the vast majority of Lets trading in Britain was being carried out in local systems covering areas up to about 20 miles across. Some people are developing methods for trading more widely within larger regions, and there are a couple of national Lets for members in particular interest communities.

When a Lets trade requires sterling to change hands as well — such as a member repairing someone's car where parts have to be bought — the seller accepts Lets for the time, and pounds for the sterling costs such as parts etc. Only the Lets part of the transaction is notified to the Lets accountant. It is perfectly acceptable too for members to charge proportions of trades in Lets and sterling as they wish — this is particularly relevant to businesses.

Transport

Offered

Caravan hire neg. *Terry* ▆▆▆▆▆

Taxi service 4B per hour + petrol *Terry & Jackie* ▆▆▆▆▆▆

Lifts by car 4B per hour + petrol *Rob* ▆▆▆

Covered 2 ton pickup with driver for transport especially to recycling depot neg. *George* ▆▆ *& Pam* ▆▆

Car washing 4B per car *David* ▆▆▆▆

Taxi and transport by van with driver 4B per hour + mileage *Dennis* ▆▆▆▆▆▆▆

Light van with driver 4B per hour + running costs, trips to London neg. trailer for rent 6B per day *Peter* ▆▆

Battery charger 6v and 12v for hire 3B per day *Peter* ▆▆▆

Huge adjustable spanner with 18 inch handle to fit nuts up to 2.25inches for hire 2B per day *Peter* ▆▆▆

Accompanying learner drivers in your own car 6B per hour *Peter* ▆▆▆

Sherpa van: with driver 6B per hour + petrol, self drive 4B per hour + petrol *Martin* ▆▆▆

Car and van clutch replacement and servicing 8B per hour + parts *Martin* ▆▆▆▆

Arc welding and fabrication 8B per hour + rods *Martin* ▆▆▆▆

Pickup with driver neg. *Eileen* ▆▆▆

Horse riding and lessons 6B per hour *Sue* ▆▆▆▆

Deliveries 4B *Daryl* ▆▆▆▆

Driving and lifts *Brian* ▆▆▆

Basic car mechanics and tuning 4B per hour + materials *Jay* ▆▆▆▆

Trailer for rent 4' by 3' 6B per day *John* ▆▆▆

Car mechanics Jon ▆▆▆ *6B per hour*

Cycle repairs 5B per hour + parts; secondhand bicycles for sale B/£ neg. *Steve* ▆▆

Car repairs and maintenance 8B per hour + parts etc *Steve* ▆▆▆

Hire of large wheel brace for vans and trucks 2B per hire, hire of torque wrench 1B per day *Steve* ▆▆▆

Car repairs and servicing - qualified 8b per hour + Parts Occasional local lifts *Martin* ▆▆▆

Wanted

Mechanic *Sheila* ▆▆▆

Welding *Sheila* ▆▆▆

Transport - occasional lifts *Muriel* ▆▆▆▆▆

Driving lessons neg. *Lucy* ▆▆▆

Welding for car and woodstove *Steve* ▆▆▆

Old bike parts and Citroen 2CV parts *Steve* ▆▆▆

Car maintenance *Emma* ▆▆▆▆▆

Car repairs and servicing of Citroen 2CV *Iona* ▆▆▆▆

-5-

A page from the Malvern Lets directory showing the transport services on offer and wanted.

Is Lets money, barter — or a measure?

This may seem an interesting but not terribly useful semantic exercise, but it is important because in the next few years increasing numbers of people will be learning about and using Lets and we need a clear way of describing it. Also in the future various aspects of Lets trading will find their way into the law courts, and while there is no case law in Britain on Lets (and as far as we know, little anywhere else either) there is a body of law on money and barter.

Some members are resolute that Lets is 'local money'. Others are in Lets because they want nothing to do with money at all, and will not use the term. Other groups consider themselves as barterers. It is likely the debate will run and run.

According to the *Oxford English Dictionary*, money is 'current coin ... metal stamped in pieces of portable form as a medium of exchange and measure of value.'

Money is generally thought of as having the following characteristics:

- it is in the form of coins or notes,
- it represents wealth,
- it is issued by a national government,
- it can be used to buy or sell goods and services, and
- it is used to measure value.

Lets only has the last two of these characteristics. When describing it we have to consider whether we should call it money when it is actually quite different from what we usually believe money to be.

On the other hand when we talk of barter many people have a vision of medieval peasants exchanging flagons of mead for bushels of oats. The essential characteristic of such transactions is that no money changes hands, and the trade is usually understood to be reciprocal. The drawback is that if the first peasant doesn't want the second peasant's oats, they don't trade. With money, the shopkeeper sells the flagons of mead for hard cash, and the customers buy using the money they earned from selling their oats.

With Lets and modern banking practice the distinctions begin to blur. When the shopkeeper sells the mead to a customer who uses a cheque or a credit card, no money in the form of hard cash changes hands. The transaction is only measured in pounds and the process shows up on a couple of bank statements. But is this barter as it is trading goods without using money?

Lets transactions follows the same process: the shopkeeper sells goods and receives a Lets cheque and the transaction shows up on two 'bank' statements.

The problem with these descriptions is that because the concept of Lets has only come into general usage so recently, we don't yet have the language to describe it clearly to those new to the concept.

In my opinion, Lets is a *measurement* and strictly speaking we should not refer to it as barter or money. The drawback of (conventional) money is that it is not just used as a unit of measurement but as a lot more. Lets, however, can only be used as a way of measuring transactions — it has no other use. It does not measure credits, debts, interest or investments. Lets units cannot be 'withdrawn' from your account, in the way that you can 'withdraw' money from a bank account.

Readers attempting to describe Lets to newcomers may find it easier to introduce it as a sophisticated barter system, then go on to make the distinction.

Is Lets a register, a bank, a club, or a classified ad column?

Lets has some of the functions of all of these. It is a register in that people sign up to it, it is a bank in that it keeps accounts and sends out statements, it is a club or association in that people have come together for mutual benefit, and it is a classified advertisement column in that it publishes notices listing goods and services people want to trade.

There are, however, aspects of all these that Lets does not share. Lets does not seek to rival the banks in their main objective of earning profit from lending money and charging interest.

Nor does Lets need to perform all the functions of a normal club or society in order to function. It does not need a constitution or a committee in order for people to trade: in its most pared-down state it merely needs a method of listing offers and wants and someone to keep the accounts.

Lets performs some of the functions of a classified column in that it lists goods and services for sale and wanted. It does not, however, need to include the advertising copy usually used to persuade people to buy. The directory can work perfectly adequately just by listing goods and services.

There is an advantage in Lets being seen as a membership club because the various laws which govern so much of our lives take a different view of activities within a members-only association as opposed to work for the general public. Selling cooked food to the public, for instance, requires inspection by environmental health officers who insist that kitchens have plastic work surfaces, insect screens etc. Selling food within a club carries no such restrictions. This is not to say that Lets is a way of circumventing quality standards, merely that Lets customers are likely to be able to see for themselves whether the cook has dirty fingernails and is the sort of person likely to add chalk and sawdust to the bread mix!

How much is the Lets unit worth?

Lets groups in the UK use a variety of ways of giving a value to their unit.

- Most opt for the simple one of tying it to the national currency. So one Stroud (as units are called there) is equal in value to one pound.

    This makes it easier for newcomers to Lets to understand the concept. This method also helps members who want to charge partly in Lets and partly in sterling to calculate clear proportions.

    The ease of charging in a mix of Lets and sterling is particularly important for businesses which have overheads which have to be paid in pounds (heating and lighting, tax, bank loans etc.). It also means that when businesses declare their Lets income for tax purposes it is absolutely clear how much it represents in sterling.

    This ease of understanding also makes it easier to persuade people to join and so the system is more likely to become widespread and an integral part of the mainstream economy — if that is what the members want.

Having a standard value also allows different systems to link up so members can trade further afield in other systems.

The disadvantage of tying Lets to the national currency is that it also ties the system to the inflation (and other problems) routinely present in the world of national currencies. When the currency inflates, this inflation is likely to affect Lets.

■ Another approach to giving Lets a value is to make it time based: so one unit is equal to an hour of time. Members have done this when a prime objective is to eliminate the differentials paid to people with different skills — everyone in the system is paid the same amount for each hour of work done.

The advantage for members who are aiming for a more equal society is that a very strict element of fairness in earnings is introduced — the babysitter's time is worth the same as the accountant's.

The disadvantages are that such measures of fairness take no account of the difference in expertise, responsibility or just attractiveness of a job. It is also likely to strongly discourage businesses from joining for it makes proportional charging very difficult. It also makes it more difficult to price goods, and causes complications when people in business have to file tax returns listing their Lets income in terms of sterling. The Brighton system uses this hour-based arrangement, and has experienced problems trading in goods. Furthermore it becomes very difficult to compare the worth of units in different systems, and presents obstacles to trading between different systems.

■ A third option is to set a ballpark figure for the unit when the system launches and then say no more about it, and let members choose their rates by seeing what people already in the directory are quoting for similar work. Thus in Newbury the New Berry is valued at about 20 to the hour, and members price themselves higher or lower using this as a rough benchmark.

The disadvantages again are that it is difficult (though not impossible) to charge in clear proportions with pounds and this can cause difficulties for businesses. In Newbury the members are happy for businesses to join, but their main aim is to increase trading among individuals and one person businesses.

One result is that it takes people entirely away from the concept of money and forces them to revalue the goods and services they buy and sell. They may not arrive at a situation where all trades have equal value, but more thought will have gone into what trades and skills are worth.

- Yet another approach is the 'fudge' introduced by the Malvern system which incorporates several of the advantages of the other methods. In Malvern the group at its launch set a ballpark figure of four Beacons for an hour of basic work. In practice most members are charging between four and ten Beacons depending on the degree of skill involved. Thus people are challenged to revalue the work they do.

But the crucial point about this method is that while the typical hourly rate in *sterling* for basic work in Malvern is about £3 to £3.50, many would argue that £4 is fairer; and thus the Beacon can be considered equivalent to the pound by members who wish it, and this connection is conveniently ignored by everyone else! It remains to be seen whether the Beacon remains inflation-proof, or whether the number of Beacons charged per hour tends to increase over time.

- An interesting aberration is to be found in Manchester, one of the UK's largest systems. There the Bobbin is valued at a pound and traded as such by most members. However an informal group of members calling themselves the Bob A Jobbers trade by valuing the Bobbin as a job. So they pay each other one Bobbin for a trade no matter how long it takes and what it involves. They do so because their primary objective in the system is to promote the sense of community created by people helping each other, and the economic considerations are secondary. But they still trade perfectly happily within the much larger Manchester system.

The author on Sparkle after receiving riding lessons from Sue Humphreys on Malvern Lets. *Photo: Mike Austin.*

Coming to a decision

When making your decision, consider your aims.

If you want to have the greatest chance of penetrating the mainstream economy with large numbers of businesses taking part, opt to make the Lets unit equivalent to sterling. If you want Lets to evolve into a network of linked systems this will help.

If your primary aim is to create a feeling of community and you are not so concerned for your system to grow large or to network with others, you might use a different method of valuation.

If your aim is that everyone should be paid the same, set a fixed rate for an hour of work. This can be consistent with both parity and non-parity systems.

It is also perfectly reasonable for a town, city or district to have several different Lets running. In Leeds, for instance, at the time of writing a time-based Lets has been operating, but other citizens there who would like the opportunities for Lets to grow bigger have been considering starting one where the unit is matched to the pound. It is perfectly proper for them to do this, and people will join the systems they wish.

How are the trades valued?

Setting the value of the Lets unit is only the first step to valuing the goods and services available.

The key principle is that members make their own decisions about how much to charge and how much they are prepared to pay.

The experience has been that however the unit itself is valued, members generally think very carefully about what to charge.

Some who are already trading in sterling simply convert their pounds price to Lets and charge accordingly. But — and this is one of the many advantages of the system — many members use very different criteria for setting their rate.

The first issue in many people's minds is that they are trading with people they know in their local community — or who know someone they know. Thus members may know something of the person they are preparing to trade with, for instance that they are finding things tight because they're unemployed, or they've just had a baby and have some heavy expenditure, or they're moving house and have some sudden high bills.

In Lets, members can be regularly influenced by what they know of each other, and charge accordingly.

A second factor is the opportunity to completely re-value what we do based on whether we *enjoy* doing it. In Newbury, Andrea Harman offers ironing (which is not her favourite way of spending her time) at a high 30 New Berries an hour while Quamrul Islam offers a range of skilled accountancy services including completing the dreaded VAT forms for 20 New Berries an hour.

Such opportunities to re-value work are of particular benefit to women, who are traditionally paid poorly in sterling. It also gives more proper recognition to those horrible jobs which are badly paid in sterling but which are vital to our existence.

Finally, it is not the job of the administrators of Lets to advise members on what to charge — the price quoted and charged should be solely the responsibility of the parties to the deal.

Why are members' accounts open for inspection?

Mainstream banks guard the privacy of their customers because the ethos is that one's financial affairs are private.

But the bank itself regulates how much money the customer can draw out and spend: either up to the sum already deposited, or in the form of loans on which interest is charged.

In Lets, individual members themselves decide how much they are to spend and it is the community of Lets members who regulate how much this can be.

This regulation is both informal and effective. There is not normally a fixed limit on minus balances; what happens is that members tend to set their own limits because the rest of the membership can see what they are spending.

Thus a member's trading position can indeed become public knowledge. But because most members have some knowledge of each other, any gossip can be beneficial. Members are likely to know that the reason Sue Smith has a high minus balance is because her boy was ill and she had to pay out for a lot of child-minding.

Knowing that has a knock-on effect, for people with a high minus balance will often find that other members make a point of offering them work which might have gone to other people.

Similarly a member with a high plus balance is likely to be approached by people keen to sell to them, for their spending will help others on the system address their minus balances.

Experience shows that publishing accounts spurs people to trade — to buy if they possess what they see as too many units, to sell if they are in minus, and to go further into minus and encourage trading if they see that other members are further in minus than they are.

In Malvern the system publishes members' opening and closing balances for a given period so everyone knows how much trading is being done and who is doing it. Other systems view the publication of all personal accounts as revealing too much information, and while the administrator will give anyone's trading balance on request, they will only publish a summary without names, and often in a graph form.

It can be argued that a person who receives unlimited interest-free credit by committing themselves to working for the community should expect the community of Lets users to know how much they are buying and selling.

Why is it so important that Lets is non-profitmaking?

Lets is a community-owned resource requiring no risk capital to set up. When entrepreneurs start businesses the conventional wisdom is that they will only be prepared to risk their time and investment if they stand to make a profit. The risks in Lets are minimal, and the fundamental economic aim is to ensure all spending relates exactly to work done or goods sold — unlike the world of pounds where much of the trading is in the currency itself which has nothing to do with actual work or goods.

The people who do the work running Lets — the accounts and the directory — get paid for their time. If they don't do it well enough, the members can find people to do it better.

The system could make a profit by charging more Lets units for administration than is actually paid to the administrators, but there is no need for it to do this. Most importantly, if it does it will start going down the slippery slope to interest payments, commissions, shares, gilts, and we might as well have carried on using sterling.

So the number of Lets units in existence is equal exactly to the amount of work done and goods sold — none of them are siphoned off for non-productive use. The amount in circulation is decided upon by the users, and once created it will be spent again in the very community in which it was born.

CHAPTER 3

Buying and selling in Lets

They are not a bargain: they are cheap because people are desperate to make a sale.
RICHARD ADAMS, *WHO PROFITS?*

P eople joining Lets are normally asked to complete an application form and pay a few pounds to register. The form is likely to ask for a specimen signature and will include a section to list offers and wants.

Your offers

Take time filling in this section: you probably have many abilities which you wouldn't normally think of offering for sale. In Appendix 1 is an 'Inspiration List' showing many of the goods and services which have been traded on Lets across the country.

To help focus your mind on what you can offer, first list all the things you might think of as work — painting and decorating, cooking, gardening, driving, or whatever. Then list other activities you *like* doing — storytelling, building models, making baskets, having a gossip with someone living alone, walking and so on.

Finally list any equipment that you own — a trailer, or some chimney sweeping brushes, an electric drill, a washing machine — and would be willing to share.

Any of these can be traded or hired on Lets — you are not limited to the services normally available in the world of sterling.

Where can you look for someone to stay in the house one morning because the gas company are coming round? Where else could you find someone who describes themselves as a 'conversationalist and dinner companion'?

How much to charge?

It is up to you to decide the rates you want to charge. You might want to charge a high rate for a service you dislike but recognise that many people want. You might want to charge a higher rate at certain times of the year (repairing a car outside in the winter is quite different from doing the same job on a warm spring morning). You may be prepared to charge a lower rate in Lets than you normally do in pounds because you are likely to be dealing with local people whom you know, rather than complete strangers. Or you may recognise that since the Lets units you'll be earning will stay in the community and probably find their way back to you, you'll charge less. You may charge less to someone who finds it difficult to make ends meet such as a single parent or a pensioner. Or you may charge more to a business using your services.

The first place to look when deciding your charges is your system's directory which will tell you what other members are charging for similar services. You don't have to ask the same, you may be more or less skilled, more or less experienced, a faster or slower worker, in greater or less need, or liking or disliking the work more. It's for you and the buyer to decide.

The experience of Lets in practice is that over time the more 'extreme' charges come into line — people charging higher rates tend to bring them down to the average because they don't want to profiteer, and those undercharging raise their prices so they do not feel they are being undervalued.

You can state in the directory that part of some deals will have to be in pounds where you have unavoidable sterling costs.

What do you want?

The second part of the form will be for your wants. To compile this section list the things you routinely pay people for — car repairs, taxi services, plumbing, takeaway meals, vegetables etc.

You'll find many people have a skill which they will provide if another member specifically requests it, but won't necessarily think to offer it in the directory.

Starting trading

When you've sent your application form in you will receive a Lets chequebook, a copy of the member's agreement (for examples of these see Appendix 2) and a directory similar to the Yellow Pages. This directory will list offers and wants with members' names, addresses and phone numbers.

You are now ready to start trading, but remember: you don't need to earn Lets units before spending them, and you trade with whom you want.

To trade you merely contact the person with whom you want to make the deal. This part of the process is like replying to an advertisement in your local paper. You specify the job you want done or are offering, you agree the price, and you assess the person's ability to do the job.

When the job has been completed, the buyer gives the seller a Lets cheque for the agreed amount, and the seller sends it to the Lets administrators. In a month or two you'll both be sent statements showing your trading balance.

Most systems charge a small number of Lets units to pay the

people who do the Lets accounts and prepare the directory, so the first item on the statement is likely to be a minus — 'provision of chequebook' — six Lets perhaps.

The following items will be the trades you have done — figures with a plus for Lets you have earned, and minuses for those you have spent. The statement will be similar to the statements you receive from a bank, except there won't be a figure deducted or added for interest, nor will there be an accompanying letter from the manager asking you to explain how you intend to pay off the unauthorised overdraft...

Your own statement may be accompanied by figures showing the trading positions of other members. Some systems will issue this in the form of a graph, others will list members' names, the amount of trading they have done and their balance. This is your opportunity to judge whether your own level of trading fits in with that of others. You may have an embarrassing slate of riches which could be used to help others reduce their minus figures. Or you might be extensively committed with a high minus figure. Do not worry — by spending you have brought wealth to others and as long as you are prepared to stay committed to working for people in Lets you are using the system as it should be used.

In practice many members set their own informal credit limits and they stop buying when they reach it. It's your responsibility, but remember: all members are likely to know what you're doing!

This is Lets at its simplest. But many systems go further than this to help people to trade. Some will mark the entries of members in the directory with an asterisk to show they particularly want to trade — for example if they are new to the system and haven't yet sold very much, or have built up a large minus.

Many run trading days or markets for members to gather and trade in person. These can be very effective when a system is starting as their great value is that they allow members to meet and assess whom they want to trade with. An effective method is to rent a hall (if possible) for Lets units, and to pay the costs by charging members in Lets units (or partly in sterling) for displaying goods and listing services. Meeting other members on neutral ground can be very helpful when deciding whether to trade with them: a casual chat with a person may help you decide whether you want them babysitting your children, for example.

Many systems combine these trading occasions with social events — an hour of trading, followed by an hour of music and tea.

What can be traded on Lets?

Anything which can be traded in pounds can be bought or sold on Lets — and because the system creates a community of local people, many members will trade services which they wouldn't want to offer to the general public.

Experience has shown that people's greatest need is for the everyday things of life which involve someone's time. Painting and decorating, car repairs, book-keeping services, babysitting, gardening, vegetables and cooked meals, simple household jobs such as putting up shelves, or feeding pets at holiday time.

A major area of trading is in repairs, for it is here that the sterling economy falls down. How often has a shopkeeper told you something isn't worth repairing because a new one would be cheaper than the repair? And how often have you gone home feeling resentful at having to throw something away which would have a long and distinguished life if it wasn't for that small widget which has broken?

The washing machine repairers on Lets should do particularly well, as should the car mechanics, clock repairers, electronics wizards, and those who sew and darn.

And Lets can be a good source of finding someone to wait in for the meter reader again when you can't find a friendly neighbour to leave a key with.

Lets encourages people to offer services they wouldn't otherwise offer: there's a world of difference between providing bed and breakfast for friends of Lets members visiting the area, and putting a sign outside the house for all comers. Many people would balk at having strangers walk through the door to use the washing machine — but a Lets member living nearby in a bedsit?

The do-anything 'slave for a day' can be particularly useful, and the person of ingenuity offering 'surprises' could make a day special for someone dear to you.

Accommodation in Peru (yes, actually offered on one system) might have only a specialist market, while haircutting is something most of us need at some time.

Can you sell Lets for pounds?

Lets is not designed to help people acquire pounds — there are far too many financial institutions purporting to do that already.

However there may be limited opportunities for selling Lets units for sterling but only between individual members.

Such deals can only really be made if there are members who are fairly wealthy in sterling and don't mind putting pounds in to help someone less well off. The deal would operate by a person who has amassed say 200 Lets units (where the unit is equivalent to £1) selling them to another member for £200.

In such a trade the pounds are treated like any other goods for sale. The buyer of the Lets units has spent £200 but has 200 Lets in their account to spend. The seller pockets £200 and their Lets balance is reduced by 200 units.

It's a private deal between the two of them and various permutations in the process are possible.

But beware. Members should ensure they don't allow the deal to devalue Lets by, for instance, selling the 200 Lets for only £150. The member's agreement (see Appendix 2) allows administrators to refuse to record transactions viewed as inappropriate — and it could be argued that a deal which devalues the Lets unit shouldn't be recorded.

Secondly, if the Lets unit is not tied to sterling there is a genuine difficulty in valuing the Lets in pounds. The same caution applies: those party to the deal should be sure that a fair arrangement is being struck.

The question of what *shouldn't* be sold on Lets is not easy. The safest approach is firstly follow the spirit of the law and not allow members to exchange anything on Lets that they couldn't sell for sterling. It would also be safest to ensure that any offers are not going to cause serious offence to your members.

Ultimately the mechanism is there to encourage trading, create work, and encourage the sense of community so lacking in today's world.

But don't let your enthusiasm run away with you — arrangements between people on a voluntary basis which are already working effectively need not be brought into Lets.

CHAPTER 4

The benefits of Lets

*Riches are psychological rather
than economic and consist of
the moderation of desires rather
than the accumulation of good
things.*
LOUIS BOUDIN

Users of Lets will experience distinct benefits which they
are unlikely to receive when dealing in sterling.

The economic benefits for members

The chief economic advantage of working with Lets is that it
opens up opportunities to trade where money in the form of
pounds isn't available, and it provides instant free credit on
demand.

Spending in Lets can either substitute for sterling, making the
scarce pounds go further, or it can allow people to buy things they
would not otherwise be able to afford and thus make life a little
more enjoyable.

For people with time and little cash, Lets can allow them to
work when there is no employer willing to hire them.

For people in work there's the opportunity to make their
pounds go further by buying goods and services for Lets, and
paying back either with their skills, or by hiring out equipment
that those with higher cash incomes are able to buy but may use

only occasionally. In Leicester a group of predominantly Asian outworkers are about to use Lets to exchange equipment and skills.

Lets also allows women to employ men with more safety, especially important for repairs or work done within the home.

In these days of anonymous communities many elderly people and those with disabilities are forced to rely on social services or charity to have small jobs done — shopping, cleaning, getting a lift so they can go out. Many people in such circumstances find it embarrassing asking for favours, but with the opportunity to pay in Lets, the relationship can become more equal. I have an elderly aunt who will ask me to do small jobs when I call: I'm pleased to do them, but sometimes they need doing more urgently than I can visit. While I would not argue that Lets should be used to pay me when I visit my aunt, they can be used to widen the opportunities to have these little (and not so little) jobs done by people who are not immediate family or friends.

Most elderly people should be able to sell on Lets as well as buy — there are few people indeed who have nothing they can do. (For people who are very seriously disabled see Chapter 12).

A HELPING HAND

Newbury Lets has a member with Parkinson's disease. According to Val Oldaker, this member thoroughly enjoys working on his allotment — but although he can do most of the tasks needed to produce his fruit and vegetables, he finds the digging too much. Joining Lets has solved the problem: he employs people to dig his allotment and pays them in New Berries. Then when he is harvesting he sells plants for Lets units.

Before joining he had to beg for favours from friends and acquaintances: now he participates more in the local economic community.

Lets can provide a halfway house for people wanting to change their work and set up on their own: they can set up easily on Lets to test the market.

Because Lets is particularly suitable for employing people to repair goods, such transactions have a double benefit. Not only is the repair more economic on Lets, but the buyer is also saved the sterling necessary to pay out for a replacement when the original may well have considerable life left in it. The fact that Lets units are available on demand and interest-free means people need not wait to acquire money, and goods needing maintenance can receive attention earlier, thereby possibly avoiding more expensive work later.

For businesses there's the opportunity to sell to a new market with free advertising provided, and in particular to sell to the increasing numbers of people who don't have the cash to buy. Businesses can also benefit by reducing their sterling overheads by buying in stock or work in Lets.

LETS AND CHILDREN

Many Lets groups have children in their systems. Some parents allow their children to use their cheque books, while other children have joined in their own name.
Daniel Winkworth (15) in Telford has been spending his Wrekins wisely: fifty of them went to buy a windsurfer which he couldn't have otherwise afforded. And when it was his turn to do the washing-up he paid a neighbour in Lets for using her dishwasher!

Cara Dobson (13) and Jessica Bingham (14) in Manchester have been even more entrepreneurial. They set up to make and sell tie-dyed T-shirts — and sold 30 for £3.50 plus 3 Bobbins each. 'I've sold 300 Bobbins worth of goods,' says Cara, who also makes handpainted giftboxes, and sugar flowers to decorate cakes. With her earnings she bought shelves and a mirror for her bedroom. 'It gives me a chance to show off my skills,' she said, 'and it helps because I don't have much money.'

The social benefits

For many people there are considerable social advantages to joining Lets.

John Healy of Newbury Lets prepares the latest batch of bread and rolls to be exchanged for New Berries. *Photo: Frank Oldaker*

Unlike a century ago, most of us now live in an anonymous world. The average household moves every seven years, and many people, particularly in their late teens and twenties, move even more frequently. The result is a world where if we do know our neighbours, we only know some of them well. In big cities a trip to the shops is unlikely to result in a chance meeting with a friend.

In the countryside where much travel is by car, casual meetings are often limited to waves from drivers passing in lanes. And many experience great loneliness which they try to combat by enrolling at evening classes or going to clubs.

Conventional money contributes to this sense of anonymity as most of our trading is with strangers and few people personally know those from whom they are buying. This, of course, is in contrast to times past when trading was seen as part and parcel of a community's social life.

Experience has shown that Lets creates, in the words of Val Oldaker, administrator of Newbury Lets, 'a mental village' — people join and become part of a community. The community can often be very extensive since Lets attracts members from across the classes and from a wide range of political, social and cultural backgrounds. This aspect of meeting with people with different outlooks is not to be underestimated.

John Rhodes of Stroud Lets says he has made more friends

in his four years of membership than he did in his whole life before.

When I interviewed people for this book most replied in a fairly deadpan way to questions about the economic benefits they found. But when asked about the social benefits, most members sat up excitedly and told of the number of friends they had made, and how their whole social life had improved.

The social networks which result can make people feel more at home in their communities. Not only do they have more people to turn to in times of need, they meet more people to chat with on the high street and in the park, and — as important — they meet a wider range of people.

One married couple found their relationship suffering because they were rarely going out as they couldn't afford to pay baby-sitters. After joining Lets they got on far better when they used Lets units to pay for someone to care for their children and they regained some sort of social life.

Such arrangements can particularly help parents who feel themselves tied to the home and children. People moving to a new area can find an instant network of contacts through their Lets membership as can people moving onto a new housing estate.

People's attitudes to money can change too; in a Lets trans-action people can often afford to be more generous as they are not eking out a scarce resource but giving recognition for work done — so they may pay more than is asked in order to be sure they are not 'exploiting' a fellow member. In the world of sterling the only way of being sure you are not exploiting people working in a big company is not to buy from them!

Trading within Lets can also be educational. At its most basic we can take up the offers of tuition in German, woodworking, guitar or cooking which members offer each other. Many members also say that trading in Lets, and getting their mind around how many Lets units are circulating, has allowed them, often for the first time in their lives, to make some sense of what is happening in the economy. Lets makes us think of money in a different way, and assessing value in Lets can help us deal with pounds in a more realistic way.

LET'S DATE!

It all started with a phone call to Jim Wallis, one of the people offering car repairs on Newbury Lets. Could he have a look at a car for its MOT? Seventy-five hours later, Jim was the 'richest' Lets member in Newbury, his riches coinciding with a time when he had little cash. So he started thinking of what to spend his Lets on. According to Jim, he had a piano accordion which he wanted to learn to play.

'Daphne advertised piano teaching and so I managed to convince her that teaching me the piano accordion would not be that different,' said Jim.

'I came round for a second lesson and stayed, and three days later I went home for my toothbrush and the rest of my possessions, and have had a marvellous time ever since. You meet such nice people on Lets!'

For her part, Daphne is also well satisfied: 'I saw Jim at a party and the next day he was giving me some composting advice for my garden. Then he persuaded me I could teach him to play the piano accordion and he invited me for a curry, and when he came for another lesson he brought a bottle of wine and stayed for somewhat longer. Then he came the next night, and the next. I joined Lets to meet interesting people and I've certainly done that!'

Jim responded: 'The thing I like most about Lets is that you get acknowledgement for favours done. I will do anyone a favour, but when it is the fifth favour fixing someone's car it can get a bit much. So I say I will charge a certain amount in Lets and it stops me becoming fed up that people might be taking advantage of me. And it stops people feeling terrible about asking me again.' And the accordion lessons?

'Oh,' said Daphne, 'they just seemed to get forgotten about!'

Economic benefits to the community

Lets is primarily local which means that as soon as a system is created it is reflecting the amount of wealth in the local community. Whereas most of the pounds we spend flow out of our communities, Lets units stay in them to benefit more and more local people.

If you ever have any doubts about how pounds flee away from us consider the traders in your town. How many of the shops, workshops, factories, warehouses and financial institutions are actually locally owned? Would the owners of supermarkets have built them if they didn't expect to get more money out than they put in?

Lets units, however, because they generally can't be used outside the town, village or city district where they originated, regenerate the local economy. They introduce a new way of exchanging goods and services when there isn't sufficient sterling available.

For instance a greengrocer buying vegetables from a local grower for Lets and selling for part Lets can use those units to pay extra staff, or have essential maintenance done on the shop. The grower might thus be able to afford to employ some extra workers at busy times, and those workers can use the Lets they earn to buy babysitting so they can go to a local restaurant which may buy from the greengrocer... In the world of sterling the shop-keeper is reliant on customers with scarce money to buy their goods which come from factories outside the area — and the shopkeeper's profit is the limit of the contribution those pounds make to the local community.

Because most work on Lets is in the form of labour and time, the systems also address a fundamental problem of national currencies. Most people would acknowledge that Britain and many other countries have too many people without work. What is surprising, though, is the way people fail to realise that if the prime aim of every business is to increase output per head that must mean people lose their jobs. Indeed the very tax regime encourages this: businesses which employ people pay more tax, but the same money going into equipment and stock is tax-deductible! Lets does not suffer from this problem: it is far easier to sell your time on Lets than to use it to buy equipment (not least because most equipment comes from far away) and thus it encourages work rather than unemployment.

Environmental benefits

As we become more and more concerned about the environmental damage we are doing to our air, water, food and soil, people are seeking ways to consume in a green way.

The attacks on our environment come from many quarters: from food factories far away, from the companies selling chemicals for every conceivable use, from the lorries and private cars pumping CO_2 into the atmosphere, and from the packaging which is filling up ever more holes in the ground.

Trading locally with local people can help fight this barrage of attacks on our (mostly) beautiful world. Paying Lets to have something repaired saves us buying a new one and (often) having it transported from a distant country with all the attendant pollution and energy use. It also means the old one doesn't need to find its way to a landfill tip.

Buying from a local shop which buys food from local producers can reduce the number of juggernauts coming into our towns to deliver to the supermarkets, and thus reduce the need for ever more roads.

Easy access to hiring equipment means we are less likely to have to buy expensive durables needing finite raw materials and energy to make.

Conventional money contributes little to promoting such environmentally-beneficial purchasing. Lets networks — when they grow large — have the potential to help us on the road (or rail) to a sustainable economy where we are not spoiling the planet for short-term gains.

CHAPTER 5

Launching a new system

Money doesn't grow on trees.

It may be an unfortunate metaphor, but launching a new system is a little like the emperor persuading the people to admire his new clothes.

We have seen that national money and Lets are, above all, a matter of confidence. Consequently the main focus in setting up a system is to create confidence in the Lets unit. After all, you're suggesting to people new to the entire concept that they do some work and receive in return this strange and intangible unit instead of hard cash.

The most effective way of doing this is to get your system trading as soon as possible, and show that it is being run efficiently.

- Try and make sure the people you work with are confident, assertive and dynamic so you create an atmosphere of enthusiasm.
- Don't try and solve every tiny problem before your launch.
- Don't add on all sorts of extra facilities to the system.
- Don't keep waiting for just a few more members before you start.

Your system needs to be trading as soon as it possibly can. Don't follow the path blazed by one system (which will remain nameless) where they researched every possible permutation of what might happen — and still hadn't started operating many months later.

There are many ways of launching a Lets network, but most systems hold some sort of launch meeting to get the ball rolling.

A grand purchase. Sandra Bruce plays her grand piano, bought for 1000 Strouds. *Photo: Polly Lyster (a Lets photographer)*

It's for you to decide what this meeting comprises, but it needs to be planned carefully.

Setting up the launch

Your first job is to find a few like-minded people who will do some of the initial development work. In most areas this should not be too difficult. The obvious place to start is to ask around your friends and acquaintances. If you cannot find people you know, try advertising on newsagents' noticeboards, in the local community centre, on a library noticeboard, via a community development organisation or self-help charity. You could even try one of the political groups — some systems have been started by local Green Parties.

Then hold a small gathering of this steering group. The first stage is to ensure your group has a reasonable grasp of the concept — to do this you could suggest they read this book.

Then set a launch date and book an easily accessible venue for a meeting. This meeting will be your formal launch. Publicise it by distributing handbills and advertisements everywhere you can think of: newsagents' boards, the council's what's on diary, local libraries, community newsletters, noticeboards in local halls, church newsletters, local cafés and pubs, the chamber of commerce, centres for the unemployed, doctors' surgeries and so on. Ask the secretaries of sympathetic organisations to write about you in their newsletters.

Produce a press release for the local newspapers, and a couple of days after sending it ring up to ensure they haven't lost it. Try and persuade them to give you extensive coverage. Some systems have made front page headlines in local newspapers. Do the same with your local radio and television stations. Be prepared to be interviewed.

Next, plan the launch. Some systems make all the decisions on the name and value of the Lets unit, subscription rates, and election of administrators at the launch meeting. In others the steering group makes all these decisions early on, and those attending the launch meeting are presented with a structure which they are invited to join. Both methods work, and it's up to you which one you adopt.

The advantage of deciding it all beforehand is that it gives you plenty of time at the meeting to explain how Lets works, and for your members to meet one another and actually begin trading.

The disadvantage is that you're not giving your prospective members much say in how their system is to run. If you've decided — say — not to peg your Lets unit to the national currency, you may put some people off, and this might have been avoided by a discussion at the meeting.

Whichever approach you adopt, you will need to have in mind specific people who would be prepared to do the administration, and who will do it well.

You will also need to be aware that a substantial part of the meeting will be spent explaining what Lets is and how it works. If you don't have anyone confident enough to do this before a packed meeting, try and find a speaker from a neighbouring system or from Letslink.

The best formula is to try and mix business with pleasure, so book a pleasant room and lay on some food and drink. It is better to book a room somewhat smaller than you anticipate needing, because a crowded room implies success in a way that the same number of people rattling about in a much bigger hall doesn't. Put together a small exhibition of newspaper cuttings and samples of chequebooks, directories, application forms, member's agreements etc., all of which are available from LetsLink. If you can, learn from the launch of Bishops Castle Lets: they booked a room in a fine pub on a Saturday night, and brought along a band to play after the business of launching the system was completed.

The launch meeting

- Get the furniture right. Conventional meetings are conducted by people on a platform who, by the physical arrangement of the hall, are seen to be 'in charge'. Lets is a community resource in which all share, so begin by laying out your chairs in a circle so the steering committee and speaker(s) are seen as 'one of us' and not 'one of them on the stage'.

- Allow people some time to gather, mentally arrive, look at the exhibition, have something to eat and drink, and mix informally. This interaction can be helped by designating someone to welcome each person as they come in, and to introduce them to someone already there — especially if they are on their own.

- Start punctually. It is more important to be courteous to those who have arrived on time than it is to be considerate to those who are late. And remember — starting late can imply you haven't quite got your act together.

- You are likely to have to do five things at your meeting.

    1 Explain what Lets is and how it works.
    2 Show that it works.
    3 Make some decisions about how your system will run.
    4 Decide who are going to do the various jobs.
    5 Get people to sign up to become members.

1 **Explaining Lets.** You should be able to cover this in about 45 minutes. A crisp presentation of 20 minutes should explain the key points. Follow this with about 20 minutes of questions to deal with more detailed issues.

2 **Showing it works.** Having explained Lets, it can be useful to show that it works in practice. An effective way is to play a game for about 20 minutes where people pretend to trade with one another. This game playing also allows people to get up and move around, fetch a cup of tea, and greet friends: it is a useful breather. A description of the game is given below.

3 **Organisation.** You now need to make some decisions. The first job (often neglected in the rush) is to decide whether to form a Lets scheme or not.

   Assuming that you do, the second job is to adopt names for the system and the Lets unit. An effective way of doing this is to 'brainstorm'. One person has a large sheet of paper and a pen, and everyone present calls out suggested names which are all written down — no matter how silly. The crucial point about a brainstorm is that people make no comment whatever about the names coming forward. Names will tumble out as people's minds are exercised and this can be when the wittiest names (which may be the most effective) are suggested.

When you have about 30 or 40 names for the system, stop the brainstorm, and ask people to list the criteria to be considered when making the decision. You may want something bright, something local, not so zany it puts off the business community, something short, and so forth. Then go through the names in turn seeing which ones receive a high number of votes. The three highest should then be discussed in the light of the criteria you have agreed, and then the meeting decides — by voting if necessary — on the one it wants.

Having decided the name of your system, you then need to repeat the process for the name of your Lets unit.

Each of these decisions can be made in about 15 minutes — the process sounds longwinded, but can be moved along quickly, and this part of the meeting can be quite entertaining and humorous.

The next decision is to give a value to the unit. The different options for this are listed in Chapter 2.

Now decide your subscription charges (in pounds and Lets).

4 The jobs. You need to decide:

- which of the core group jobs are to receive a Lets payment;
- who is going to do the various jobs; and
- when the first directory will go to press.

This part of the meeting is slightly tricky: members will want to be sure the administration lies in capable hands, but at this stage are unlikely to know people well enough to make an informed judgement of whether they are capable of doing the jobs. (Beware of the people who get all enthusiastic over a new exciting project and then quickly lose interest...) You could get round this by deciding in advance the composition of a steering committee to undertake these jobs or you could hold another meeting a couple of weeks later to decide. Neither method is ideal, but you need to be very careful who does these key jobs, for success will rest on how well your directory is produced, and whether the accounts are kept accurately and efficiently. A description of the different jobs is given in Chapter 6.

5 Signing up the members. During the meeting there will be people who have decided to join; others who will want to think about it; while yet others will have decided to join, but want some time to think of what services to offer.

Your most important job is to sign up as many of these people as you can. Make sure you have a membership table with forms available, and open a bank account. If you haven't chosen a name before the meeting use a name just for the bank account, and change it later if necessary.

It is best to accept membership applications with names and addresses and subscriptions, and allow people to send in their wants and offers later in time for the directory. Try and avoid people taking forms away to think about; get them to sign up immediately if you can, or you risk losing them.

PLAYING GAMES

An effective way of showing that Lets does indeed work is to play a game where people pretend to trade with each other using Lets. The game works like this: give sheets of paper and pens to everyone present, and form a Lets unit by giving it a name. *Do not give it any sort of value:* indeed do not mention the value of it at all at this stage.

Then ask everyone present to write down two or three services they could offer and require on Lets and invite them to price them in the Lets unit. Ask them to pass the sheet of paper onto the next person and write down the same wants and offers again. As the sheets circulate, the group will end up with multiple copies of the same directory.

Next, ask people to seek out those whom they wish to trade with, to pretend to do the trade, and agree a Lets price. But... tell them they can't trade unless they have already earned Lets units to spend. They quickly reach an impasse.

This is the first lesson from the game. It is now apparent that Lets only works when people create the Lets units by spending them.

So tell them to start trading now by creating the units. When the trade has been agreed the seller comes to a member you have designated as the 'banker' who records the transactions.

You, as the facilitator of the game, also trade during this early stage — but you only buy and you don't sell (say you're too busy if anyone asks you to do a job). *And you buy extensively.* After a few minutes you withdraw from spending and go and get a cup of tea...

The next stage is to stop the game momentarily and read out everyone's trading balance but without any comments about them. Trade again for a few minutes and then call a halt to the proceedings and run through the lessons the game has shown.

1 We've had the first lesson: Lets only works if a lot of people spend before they've earned.
2 Lots of trading has been done *even though no one knew the value of the Lets unit:* people managed to make deals nevertheless. Thus, those attending can see how much trading is likely to be possible when the system is up and running and the value of the unit is clear.
3 Even though you disappeared halfway through the game leaving a large minus figure, no one lost out, *and the trading continued.*
4 The final lesson, of course, is that people had fictitious cars fixed, bathrooms redecorated, lifts provided, typing done, and vegetables planted with no conventional money changing hands.

The directory

A fortnight or so after your launch meeting you should have the directory ready to go to press. The trading can't start until this directory is circulated, so having it available sooner rather than later is essential. But don't be disheartened if it takes longer to produce than you anticipate. The directory is a major piece of work, and even if the person responsible is used to producing such publications, producing anything new can be time consuming. When it is published send it to all members, and produce at least as many again to distribute to prospective members — the directory is likely to be your best piece of publicity material.

Congratulations: you've started up a Local Exchange Trading System!

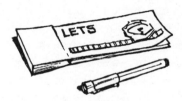

CHAPTER 6

Efficient administration

*If only all banks were this
sensible.*
WESTERN DAILY PRESS

S ince money and Lets are both built on confidence, members
will want to be satisfied that the administration is being
done well. A poorly produced directory, late and inaccurate
accounts, and letters not replied to all conspire to make prospective members have doubts about the value of being involved. Such
sloppiness also puts off existing members: one very committed
Lets trader on a successful system confessed she was *very* unim-
pressed when she discovered that her statements omitted the
crucial minus figure to show she was actually in commitment
when she thought she was in credit!

The second most important characteristic is simplicity. It's
very easy to add extras to Lets: some can indeed be very effective,
but they often mean extra work, and sometimes take you down
paths you don't intend to go. So at least in the early stages concentrate on the essential needs.

There are several jobs to do to run a Lets network:

- the accounts need to be updated and the chequebooks
  distributed;
- the directory needs to be produced and distributed;
- the membership records need to be kept;
- a treasurer is needed to handle the sterling; and
- a secretary is needed as a contact point for inquiries.

Other jobs which help the system to function but are not

strictly essential are the organisation of events, publicity, mediation, helping members to trade, and editing a newsletter.

These jobs take varying degrees of time, so it is reasonable for the more onerous ones such as doing the accounts and editing the directory to be paid in Lets units — these being debited from members' accounts.

The people doing these jobs, who are generally referred to as the management or core group, should meet fairly often in the early stages, perhaps every week or fortnight, and then less frequently as the system becomes established. But *beware of meetings:* they are needed to share work out and to make decisions, and for enjoying oneself! Don't have them for the sake of it, and try to make them enjoyable occasions. The meetings should be open to all members: the organisers should have no secrets from the other members. Generally, few members are likely to attend these meetings, and those that do can often be persuaded to become more involved.

Choosing the administrators

People can find their way into jobs in Lets via a number of routes.

- They might have been the founders, so people who join after them are presented with their presence as a *fait accompli*.
- They can be elected at a meeting of the membership.
- They might be appointed by a meeting of the core group.
- If the particular job is to be paid (such as directory editor or accounts administrator) members can tender for it.
- Or, as is more likely as a system forms, people just volunteer.

All these options have advantages and disadvantages. If members don't have the opportunity to choose the administrators they may not feel so committed. On the other hand many members do not care who is doing the administration as long as it is done well. They are perfectly happy for others to take the responsibility for choosing who should do it.

When elections are conducted properly they can be time consuming since members who don't come to meetings should have an equal opportunity for their vote to be recorded.

Appointing people can leave some members feeling that they

were not given a say, or that the wrong choice was made. Leaving it to volunteers can be very quick and easy, but you are at risk of the jobs going to the 'all enthusiastic at first, but then lose interest' brigade.

Whichever route you choose, make sure the responsibilities of the administrators are clearly set out and that there is a clear procedure for removing an administrator whose work is not up to the mark or replacing someone who resigns.

The limits of responsibility

The administrators need to be sure of the extent of their responsibilities, and the member's agreement (see Appendix) lays out a bare framework. But it is easy for administrators to exceed their duties, though often with the best of intentions. The administrator of one Yorkshire system declared that if the gun shop in his city applied to join, he would refuse to admit them. It might be that this is a defendable position under the terms of the membership agreement: 'The administrator may, in consultation with the management group, decline to record an account or an entry of goods and services for legal *or other reasons.*' An administrator could argue that increasing access to guns in a city diminishes the sense of community, increases fear, and could seriously offend existing members. But it is an arguable point. Banning controversial offers and wants from inclusion is exactly the area where administrators may get into trouble and they must be sure any such decisions have the support of the membership.

Refusing membership to a gun shop or the local soft porn merchant may well gain the support of members, and after all, these shops could start up their own system. Administrators faced with decisions which may excite controversy should consult their management group, and possibly the stewards (see below), and ensure they report back to members on the action they have taken so it can be challenged.

Paying the administrators

Some of these jobs can be fairly time-consuming, particularly editing the directory and maintaining the accounts. The work of the treasurer, secretary, events organiser etc. tends to take less time.

Each system will have to decide whether these jobs should be paid. 'Voluntary' organisations are continually wrestling with this issue as unpaid volunteers find themselves increasingly working beside salaried staff. Organisations pay people for a variety of reasons — it helps maintain continuity, it is said to attract a higher calibre of people, it encourages 'professionalism', it recognises that the work may *deserve* payment, and so on.

So how do you decide who is paid for Lets administration, and how much? First, there is no reason whatever to pay people in sterling — all payments should be in Lets (except to reimburse expenses that have to be paid in pounds). Second, it is important that the payment is for work done: it is not a distribution of profits, for Lets is a community resource which is non-profit-making.

In addition to paying your administrators for their ongoing work once the system is established, you may want to consider paying them for setting up the system in the first place.

To pay your workers you first need to set up a 'system account'. This is simply an administration account listed in the same way as any member's account is listed. Cheques are paid out of it to people doing the work, and Lets units come into it from the members — as a surcharge on transactions or by subscription.

Although the system account operates as though it was just a member's account, there is one crucial difference. For when members create Lets units which they haven't earned, they do so by making a commitment to doing some work on Lets at some time. If the system account creates credits by paying Lets units to administrators which haven't been paid in by the members as a whole, there is no individual making that commitment. This issue becomes particularly important if you want to pay people for setting up the system. This needs careful thought, for paying a lump sum of Lets units when there are only a few members will immediately show a very large minus on the system account. It would be rather akin to a new hairdressing salon opening and charging £20,000 for the first haircut because it cost £20,000 to set the business up.

Calderdale Lets has managed to pay several hundred 'Favours' for the costs of development without a serious debit, whereas others find their system accounts are heavily in minus just from paying running costs. A sensible approach would be to reckon on recouping your set-up costs over five years or so — as any business should.

So the members need to be clear how they want their system account to operate. Is it invoice-led? That is, it pays out to administrators (according to a formula) and if it goes into heavy minus, so be it. Or is it managed so it never goes into minus — or at least only temporarily and only to a limited extent?

The answer to the question of whether it matters, seems to be that it matters *if the members think it matters.*

In Brighton members are concerned at the way 'The Administration' are sucking in everyone's wealth! In Totnes members appear not to be concerned. In Manchester a subcommittee sat down rather like a council rate-setting meeting and pruned or cut various items in order to bring the account back into balance.

Nevertheless there are some guidelines:

■ Be cautious about using your system account to pay people for development work such as setting up, giving talks and arranging meetings. Such payments are very likely to overload the account in the early days.

■ Introduce some equality by deciding that administrators are only paid after they've done a certain number of hours per month for free — thus the treasurer and distribution people are likely to be voluntary jobs, while the *extra* hours needed for doing the accounts or editing the directory are paid.

■ Try to resist having the account just paying out on invoice: fix the cost of the job, and pay out on that, and this will make it more controllable.

■ If your system account is heavily in minus, your members may not care, for these credits will be flowing around the system, and members will be earning from them. They will represent wealth which has been created. But you never know when members — and particularly prospective members — may interpret such figures as a sign of poor administration and lose confidence in Lets as a result.

■ Finally, keep monitoring the account so the administrators are aware how it is being run.

While it is generally accepted in Lets that the accounts administrator should be paid by some sort of levy on transactions or the subscription, some activists believe the production of the directory should be hived off and, in effect, privatised. This method results in the system account only paying the accounts administrator, and members subscribing separately to receive the directory. The advantage of this is that only people who really want the directory receive it. The disadvantage is that few subscribers may mean a poor return for the editor (who may then be reluctant to do the necessary work), and until Lets includes every shop in the high street, all members will need to see a directory in order to trade at all.

The treasurer

No matter how much you try to operate without using sterling, you'll face some costs which have to be met in pounds.

Phone calls, stamps and photocopying costs are likely to be your main ones, and with careful budgeting it should be possible to service a member for between £6 and £10 a year — and certainly not more.

Treasurers of Lets do the same job as the treasurers of any local clubs: they open a bank account (preferably with a bank or building society which consider ethics as well as profits) and record the money coming in and going out. The treasurer can't create sterling as the other members can create Lets units. And at the end of the year s/he needs to produce the accounts so members can see what has been spent, and whether any savings need to be made or the subscription fee reviewed.

As in all such organisations, it is better for the bank account to require two signatures.

The directory editor

Your directory is likely to be your most effective form of advertising Lets and without a method of communicating wants and offers, members will find it difficult or impossible to trade.

The best directories are those which are designed to be kept by the telephone and where the entries are short and sweet. A4 folded to A5 is a comfortable size. The directory will look best if it is desk-top published on a home computer (commercial typesetting is likely to be too expensive). If you don't have a computer buff in your system when you start, photocopied typewritten sheets will do the job, and as your system expands it is likely that a person experienced in DTP will come forward.

There are as many ways of ordering the entries as there are versions of Lets, but think how people are likely to use the directory. Some will thumb through from cover to cover to see what they can do — for them the order of things is less important.

Others will be looking for a particular service, so grouping similar offers and wants is useful. It is also useful to mark 'short life' entries in the directory so the editor knows to remove them after a time.

The best approach is to divide the directory into subjects, each divided into offers and wants. List the entries with prices where people have included them, and the member's name. Specify whether prices are per hour or for the job, and allow people to state that sterling may be charged as well — e.g. '20 Lets plus materials'. When your system grows larger it can be useful to include an area code by each entry so readers can see if an offer is from someone in their immediate locality. Some entries are more useful if supplemented by an indication of when someone is available — for example for lifts.

It's down to you whether you allow the announcements to expand away from simple listings to become advertisements. An entry 'Ironing, six Lets per hour, Robin Thompson' takes up less space (and therefore fewer pages and fewer trees) than when expanded to 'Careful ironing by dedicated ironer' etc. You could charge for advertising, either in Lets or sterling, to ensure the directory is not too expensive, but ask yourself: does the world really need more advertising?

You should also decide whether you will include entries under more than one heading. The advantage is that offers and wants are more likely to be taken up; the disadvantages are that the directory will consume more paper, and it is difficult to keep track of where all the entries are when the time comes to change or delete them.

The directory should open with a short description of how Lets operates, with advice on how to trade, and the names and phone numbers or addresses of the administrators. Leave room for announcements about Lets events and don't forget to include an address and phone number for new members to contact. It is also useful to include a paragraph reinforcing the fact that Lets only works if people create the Lets units by spending them before they have them. You cannot remind people of this too often!

Include a page with members' telephone numbers or addresses, although this is best placed on a separate sheet in the directory so it is removable. You may decide to make the directory available to non-members as part of your advertising material, but your members may feel that such copies should have phone numbers removed. Your member's agreement may prohibit organisers and other members from making membership lists public. The Data Protection Act (see Chapter 11) also imposes restrictions on releasing this type of information when held on computer.

You will need to decide the frequency of publication. This can be anything between every other month and every six months, depending on how much the membership is changing. If you are attracting ten or more members a month, then publishing every two months may be appropriate; a slower rate of joining may mean publishing every quarter or even just twice a year. You are likely to find that producing the directory is expensive in time, Lets units and sterling, so consider this very carefully. And if you don't decide on a schedule it can be useful to include the deadline for the next issue so members know when to send in changes to their entries.

The newsletter

A directory published every few months can be supplemented more frequently by a newsletter. It's better desk-top published, but can be typed, and is useful to publicise new members, directory changes, offers and wants with a short life span, information about how the system is operating and news from systems further afield. If the editor is paid with Lets units from the system account, this is likely to mean (in a small system) either that members will pay a high Lets fee, or the account will go heavily into minus.

There's no reason why the newsletter can't be run as a 'stand alone' operation with members subscribing in Lets for copies.

The accounts administrator

Don't be intimidated by this part of the work; it's not as bad as it seems.

The Lets accountant keeps the record of members' addresses and phone numbers, produces and distributes the chequebooks, records the transactions after members have traded, and distributes statements of accounts.

There are two ways of keeping the accounts: in a book or on a computer. Do not allow the computer buffs to tell you that you absolutely must have a computer with a spreadsheet package, phenomenal amounts of RAM and goodness knows what else. (In May 1994 some 40 per cent of Lets in the UK were not using computers to do their accounts). If you have a member with a computer able to keep the accounts take up the offer with alacrity. However, be sure the person can do the accounts professionally and that there is a back up system so if s/he moves away or has a computer crash, there is someone else who can retrieve the situation. There is specific software available for the accounts — see 'Computerised accounts' below.

If you don't have a member with a computer, buy a ledger from a stationer.

You may feel that when you have attracted over 100 members who are each doing several trades per month, a computer would

On the following pages:
The information sheet and booking form produced by Calderdale Lets. It includes a description of how the system works, the Members' Agreement, and a short summary of some of the services available. The space for the directory entries specifies a maximum size of 40 characters as Calderdale uses the computer program 'nLets' which has this limitation.

Local Exchange Trading System

LETS...

Allows us to use our skills and time to benefit each other and the community in

Calderdale

Local Exchange Trading System

Some questions answered

How do I decide what to charge ? The amount charged is decided between the two people making the exchange. Initially we suggest that you can think of a FAVOUR as being roughly equal to a pound, though its value is determined by the parties to each trade.

How do my payments get credited ? You send or take your credit slips to any one of the listed points. They are then entered into the computer system that is used for system administration.

How can I find out my current balance ? You can ask at any time for details of your current balance or that of anyone else in the system.

What if I have no skills to trade ? We believe that everyone has skills to offer and would be happy to help you identify those you could offer through the system.

What if I don't have a phone ? We suggest that you use the number of a friend or neighbour so that you can be contacted more readily.

What do I do to join ? Just complete the form, detach it and send it off (do remember to include your registration fee). You will receive a credit book and a list of the current offers and requests in the system.

Some further current entries

3 Business and Office Services ★ Book-keeping/Accounts ★ Computer Consultancy & Training ★ Computer Programming/Analysis/Advice ★ Copywriting 5F p/h ★ Data Recovery ★ Law Work up to Litigation ★ Marketing Advice 5F p/h ★ Organisational & Management Advice/Help ★ Press Releases 5F p/h ★ Typing ★ Wordprocessing & DTP (posters etc) ★ Wordprocessing/DTP/Spreadsheets

24 Wanted ★ 4 × 6 foot fluor lights complete ★ Babysitting (woman) ★ Basic car maintenance tuition (Toyota) ★ Beautiful/eccentric objects however big ★ Bicycle repairs ★ Bodywork maintenance – Car not person! ★ CD player ★ Chair needs caning ★ DIY/Gardening ★ Dog sitting ★ Double bed + mattress ★ Dressmaking/Alterations ★ Driving lessons ★ Fruitwood/Hardwoods for turning ★ Gardening/walling/fencing ★ Gas fitter ★ Heavy Duty car battery (pillars) ★ Help required to deliver leaflets ★ Help with transport – Van or Trailer ★ Household repairs/DIY ★ Land for 'Mobile Home' ★ Lively folk dancing ★ Old huts etc for chickens/goats ★ Piano lessons ★ Plastering; Small ceiling & patches ★ Plumbing ★ Radio/cassette player repair ★ Regular good bread loaves ★ Shirt ironing approx 1 load per week ★ Shrubs and other perennials ★ Typing services/printing/phone answering ★ Vacuum cleaner ★ Woodworking tools/machinery

Local Exchange Trading System

What is It?

A Local Exchange and Trading System is basically a barter system. It helps people in the community to exchange skills and services. But it is more sophisticated, bigger, more effective. LETS schemes are based on a successful scheme pioneered by communities in British Columbia.

Unlike a barter system, working one to one, LETS allows members to build up credit with one member and spend it with another.

Among its many advantages Calderdale LETSystem:-

* Helps to share skills to support the local community

* Is run and managed entirely by its members

* Saves resources

How does it work?

Calderdale LETSystem is a voluntary, not for profit, group run and managed with the cooperation of its members. We have a core group, open to all, which helps with the day to day running of the system.

Trading is done in units of exchange which we call FAVOURS. LETSystem members are given a credit book and sent a regularly updated directory of the skills and services offered by members. This allows you to pay for services in FAVOURS and your account is debited accordingly. No interest is charged or paid on debits or credits.

Members call up the services they require or visit shops or businesses in the system.

Who can join?

Anyone in Calderdale can participate in the system whatever their skills and abilities.

Whether they are an individual or a business, large or small, members need not restrict themselves. One may offer graphic design and dog walking another ironing, plumbing and book-keeping.

What will it cost me?

To cover the cost of stamps, paper etc the first years joining cost is:- 5.00 pounds (unwaged/low waged) - 12.00 pounds (waged/salaried) depending on how much you can afford. In addition 10 FAVOURS are deducted from each account on registration, this is used to pay the people who help produce the newsletter and carry out the necessary admin jobs.

Benefits to the local community

Calderdale LETSystem offers an incentive to people to use local services and shops, thus stimulating the local economy and helping the community to thrive and prosper.

People may use the system as much or as little as they wish and can choose to charge in any combination of FAVOURS and pounds.

The system offers opportunities to develop new and useful skills and create new social networks.

A selection from the domestic and family section of our newsletter.

★ Childcare (babysitting) ★ Dogs walked ★ Gardening ★ Law work up to Litigation ★ Murals (nursery, bathrooms etc) ★ Occasional cat-sitting ★ Pets fed/talked to in your absence ★ Plants watered in your absence ★ Portrait photos for family/acting/C.V.s ★ Reading aloud ★ Reading books to people ★ Sat night babysitting 3F p/h ★ Surprises ★ Washing ★ 2 Extra pairs of hands when needed ★ Babysitting 9:30–15:00 3F p/h

Calderdale LETSystems — Membership form

If you have any questions or want any advice about completing this form – ring LETShelp ▶

Please remember to make cheques/p.o.s payable to Calderdale LETSystem

I enclose the following amount in £ sterling

Joining fee	:	5 pounds unwaged/low waged / 12 pounds waged/salaried
Donation	:	
Total	:	

We need £ sterling to pay for postage & photocopying etc

Any surplus is used to develop the system further and support the creation of a community fund.

NB 10 Favours is also deducted from each account on joining to pay for admin work - in Favours.

Yes I would like to join Calderdale LETSystem and agree to the rules overleaf.

Fill in the name and address that you wish the account, statements and newsletter to be sent to.

Name...

Address...

....

Post Code.............. Phone No. ....

Signature .... Date ..../ ....../ ......

This is the signature you will use when you make out credit notes.

Please use your Post Code as it will help us to sort entries.

The rules overleaf are important, so please do read them first.

For admin use

£	A/c opened	Credit book	Date rec'd	A/c number	User name
	Newsletter	Entries	/ /		

✂ - ✂

Local Exchange Trading System

How do I complete an entry?

These are sample entries.

offers ++ requests ---	Description (Max 40 Characters – inc spaces)	No of issues	No of characters
++	Gardening/Digging/Weeding 4F p/h neg	3	35
--	Help with housework by elderly man	2	34
++	Fitted kitchens & Wiring	3	24
++	Good Catering for parties 6F p/h + ing	3	37
--	Nice home for small pony – not rideable	3	39

The newsletter and statements are printed together and any new offers/wants to be included in them should reach us by:-

Newsletter no 2   30/7/93
Newsletter no 3   1/10/93
Newsletter no 4   3/12/93

Please note that information received late will be held for the next newsletter.

WHAT SHALL I DO NOW?
Fill in the enclosed form with a cheque or postal order
(Make sure you complete all sections)
payable to CALDERDALE LETSystem.
Send it to:-
Calderdale LETSystem,

Everyone has skills to offer

Calderdale LETSystem - Members agreement
(The fine print)

The Calderdale LETSystem is based on members personal commitment to each other and to the wider community. Confidence to extend trust or credit to members rests on the undertakings made in adopting and assenting to this Membership agreement of the Calderdale LETS group.

1/......The Calderdale Local Exchange and Trading System "LETSystem" is a non-profit membership club whose rights and authority are vested in the Council of all its members who delegate that authority at each AGM to a Management Group. The AGM will appoint an Advisory Group of 3 persons, not members of the Management Group, to arbitrate/conciliate in case any member is aggrieved by a Management decision.

2/......The LETSystem provides an information service through which members can offer and seek goods and services, and maintains central records of their transactions for the convenience of members.

3/......Members agree to the LETSystem holding their personal data on computer and to the disclosure to other members only of those details relevant to transactions, ie name, membership number, balance of commitments and total number of transactions.

4/......Members may give or receive from each other credit, recorded in the agreed Calderdale LETSystem unit of currency known as a FAVOUR.

5/......Only the account holder can authorise the transfer of units from their account to another members account.

6/......No money is deposited or issued. Any transaction maybe on a part cash basis but only FAVOURS are recorded in the LETSystem accounts.

7/......All LETSystem accounts start at zero. Members are not obliged to be in receipt of any credit before issuing another member with credit from their account, subject to any debit limit that may be set by the Management Group.

8/......All transactions are voluntary between individual members and no individual is obliged engage in any transaction whatsoever with other members. Before leaving the LETSystem however, those with commitments outstanding are obliged to balance their account.

9/......Any member is entitled to know the balance and number of transactions of any other member. The Management Group may also publish the balances and no of transactions of all accounts.

10/......No interest is charged on balances. The Management is authorised to charge joining and renewal fees in FAVOURS and/or sterling on a cost of service basis, and to levy service charges on members accounts at rates agreed at the members Council AGM.

11/......The LETSystem administrator, in consultation with the Management Group, may decline to record an account or goods or services entry considered inappropriate for legal or other reasons.

12/......The LETSystem publishes a list of goods and services offered by members but no warranty or undertaking as to the value, condition or quality of goods or services offered is expressed or implied by virtue of the introduction of members to each other.

13/......Members are responsible as individuals for their own personal tax liabilities and returns. The LETSystem has no authority, obligation or liability to report to the tax authorities, nor to collect taxes on their behalf.

14/......Members have the right and are encouraged to attend Council and Management Group meetings, and to participate in decision making on the basis of one person one vote. Members have the right of appeal to the Advisory Group on all Management decisions.

15/......The Management Group or its delegate may seek satisfaction from a member whose activity is considered contrary to the interests of the membership and may suspend membership in the case of delinquent accounts and remove or deny membership at its discretion.

16/......The Management Group may introduce such rules as, from time to time it deems appropriate, however in all such cases no change to this agreement shall have effect until agreed by a 2/3 majority voting at an AGM or extraordinary meeting for which a minimum of 28 days notice has been given to members.

17/......Members agree to be bound by the terms and conditions of this agreement.

Newsletter Entries

Please include the following entries in the next newsletter

offers ++
requests — Description (max 40 Characters)

No of issues

offers ++ / requests — Description (max 40 Characters)	No of issues

Complete this section using one line per entry
Enter .++ to indicate offers
-- to indicate requests
The limit of 40 characters includes spaces and any charge in FAVOURS that you want to make.

You can have as many entries as you need, please use another sheet if necessary but please use the same format.

Your name/phone no will appear additionally on each entry.
If you do not have a phone to help people get in touch with you more easily it may be useful to quote a friends number - by arrangement!

No of issues
The maximum number of issues that an entry will appear for is 3 (three).
You can add, alter, renew or delete entries at any time.

When you have completed this form dont forget to sign it ! send it to :-

Calderdale LETSystems

This leaflet printed on 100% recycled paper.

be useful. By then you are very likely to have attracted someone with the necessary equipment, and if you haven't, a call to other local community groups is likely to turn up a computer which you can go and use. But do not worry about this too much, for up till the early 1980s hundreds of thousands of transactions were routinely recorded by banks without access to computers.

One real advantage of a computer is that it allows you to keep easy track of how much trading is being done. This can be very useful when you need to demonstrate to prospective members how effective Lets can be.

It shouldn't be necessary for systems to buy their own computers. They are an unnecessary expense, and instead of spending (and raising) large sterling sums to profit a company far away, use Lets to employ people locally.

There are a variety of ways of presenting the accounts. A crucial component of Lets is that members can know each others' balances, but the members will need to decide exactly how this information should be presented. Most systems send the member's own account details out, but there are some differences in how other members' details are given.

In Manchester and Malvern, members receive statements showing everyone's trading position — amount sold and earned, and the balance — and with everyone's name plain to see. Other systems — such as Calderdale — publish diagrams showing balances, but with no names. When Totnes, for the first time, published all accounts with names the general reaction was 'So what?' Members concerned about their own balances seemed to know their own trading position as they kept their own records, while other members were apparently unconcerned.

While there is general agreement that an member can inquire of the administrators for details of a specified person's account, some systems believe it is an intrusion of privacy to publish all balances with names as a matter of course.

The argument for publishing balances with names is that this helps members realise it is perfectly acceptable for them to go into minus balance because they see that others are doing so. They can also make a point of offering work to people needing to earn, and can gain a picture of how much someone is in demand. There is also the strong argument that since Lets provides interest-free credit on demand, the community is entitled to know what people's commitments are.

However, publishing the accounts takes time, energy and money — both Lets and sterling — and not publishing might encourage people to inquire more closely into what is going on and thus take more interest in the administration.

But one important caveat: members have agreed in the Members Agreement (see Appendix) to their accounts being revealed to other members — *not* to the general public.

Computerised accounts

Computer programs suitable for Lets have been developed in recent years as the systems have grown. The most widely used is 'nLETS' for systems using IBM-compatible machines. Other programs for Apple Macs and to meet the needs of multiple systems linked together have had less field use, and you are advised to contact LetsLink (see Appendix) for more details of these.

At the time of writing there is no program available for Amstrad 256 WP non-IBM compatible machines, nor one specifically for Windows.

nLETS

nLETS has been written by Richard Knights of Totnes Lets for use on IBM compatible PCs and can be used with or without Windows. It extends a program developed by Lets designer Michael Linton so it is simpler to use and doesn't require dBase.

The program:

- maintains the list of members' names and addresses, date of joining and their level of trading;
- collates offers and requests and produces the directory;
- does double entry book keeping for the Lets units;
- analyses and makes graphs showing trading levels;
- can manage up to 11 separate systems;
- can output a separated file for importing into a DTP.

nLETS requires 640K of RAM, a hard disk is strongly advised and it will run in colour or black and white. The program is best run in conjunction with a DTP which can dramatically improve the quality of the printouts. One drawback of nLETS is that it will

LETS BARTER

Advertise Your Services, Goods, and Wants in the LETS BARTER Directory.

Name:

Address:

Postal Code:

Tel: (Home)
(Work)

The directory is issued every two months. If you want any entries to appear for a limited only, please indicate the time limit. Otherwise your entries will continue to appear in the directory.

Goods and services can be offered entirely in Beacons, or in a combination of Beacons and Sterling, the latter covering the cost of any materials.

If you want more ideas on what to offer please ask for a skim list.

SERVICES OFFERED	Beacons	£

SERVICES WANTED	Beacons	£

GOODS OFFERED	Beacons	£

GOODS WANTED	Beacons	£

Remember to complete the application form overleaf.

LETS BARTER

Membership Application Form

I would like to join Malvern LETS BARTER.

I enclose an annual membership fee of £____ * Cash / Cheque
NB: £8.00 waged / £6.00 low/unwaged (delete as applicable)

Name:

Address:

Postal Code:

Tel: (Home)
(Work)

I agree to the conditions of the Members Agreement, and do not object to my membership and account details being held on computer records. I also consent to the distribution of those details to all other members of LETS BARTER.

* I understand that four Beacons will be deducted from my account for each book of ten cheques issued to me.

Signed :

(This will be your specimen signature for administration of the system.)

Please return to : LETS BARTER
c/o Only Natural, 99B Church Street, MALVERN, WR14 2AE

For office use only

Chequebook sent

Acknowledgement   Directory

LETS Account number

Subscription received   Payable   Renewal Date

The membership application form produced by Lets Barter at Malvern. The form for directory entries (shown here) is printed on the reverse: this can be distributed separately for updating the announcements.

only accept directory entries of up to 40 characters. It costs £30 from LetsLink.

Richard provides a back-up service and likes members to trial the programme before deciding whether to purchase.

MLETS

A further program under development is MLETS, designed to allow several systems to be run from the same computer, and for members of each to trade with one another — what is known as 'multiLETS'. MLETS is suitable for IBM compatible machines, and does not require Windows. At present it doesn't compile the directory (for which nLets can be used) but does give an integrated multiLETS accounts system.

MLETS:
- manages members' names and addresses and accounts;
- does double entry book keeping within and between each system;
- cannot compile the offers and requests and cannot be used to produce the directory.
- If you want to separate the directory editing from the accounts, the directory can be produced on a standard DTP package or database.

LLETS

This programme, written by David Wardle of Malvern, is available just to keep the Lets accounts. LLETS is suitable for IBM compatible machines and will run on 512K of RAM and needs only a floppy disk.

LLETS:
- maintains membership records and accounts;
- prints cheques and statements;
- does not produce graphs of trading or membership.

David recommends trying the program before deciding to purchase. LLETS costs £30 direct from David — address in Appendix 4.

There are also commercial programs designed for home accounts which can be used for running Lets.

Accounts on paper

The Lets accounts can be kept very simply in a standard cash book. Use a double page for each member and head up the columns across the page as follows: date of cheque, who the cheques are from or to, Lets units spent, Lets units received, and balance. Sending the statements out is easy, as the system in Exeter discovered: their Lets accountant Mick Cole just photocopies the accounts pages and pops them in an envelope!

CHEQUEBOOKS, PHONE CALLS OR SCRAPS OF PAPER?

The object of the chequebooks is to ensure the person doing the accounts receives the information needed about each transaction. The banks which handle millions of transactions find that pre-printed cheques with spaces for specified information are effective. Lets groups could use the phone — members just ring into the Lets accountant and leave a message on an answering machine. Or they could just write the record on a piece of paper which they send in.

My advice is, *don't*. Scraps of paper are easily lost, and people can find it easy to leave out a vital piece of information — like who the Lets units are to be transferred to. And messages on answering machines can't really be relied on either: the message can be rubbed out too soon, the machine may beep at the wrong time, or the member may think they've phoned, but actually forgot to ring back when they found the line was engaged. Some members may not have a phone, and others feel reluctant to leave messages on answering machines. Using cheques is more likely to make the system operate efficiently, will make it look more efficient and can help build confidence.

Frequency of statements

There is no easy answer to the question of how frequently the accounts should be distributed. A normal bank statement is sent out so account holders know how much interest they owe, to avoid unapproved overdrafts, and to ensure all entries have been made properly. But there's no interest due on Lets accounts and 'overdrafts' don't matter. The best answer is to judge how much trading is being done. Little trading means intervals of a few months, frequent trading could mean a statement being sent more often. The one proviso is that the statements should go in the same mailing as the directory and any other correspondence, or you're making needless work for yourselves stuffing envelopes.

The distributor

Your mailing operation is an opportunity to move away from sterling into a Lets transaction. You *could* take your envelopes down to the post office and pay in scarce pounds for the stamps. But a more imaginative way is to pay members in Lets to distribute to those members living near one another. The first time this is likely to be time-consuming, but then the deliverer is likely to get into a set pattern and will save time. It is probably best to use the post for letters going to more isolated members.

The secretary

In addition to the above, there is a series of small jobs which help keep the system running sweetly. A person to respond to inquiries from prospective members, who gives or organises talks to local organisations, clears the post-box, chases the directory editor, organises the meetings and ensures the tea is made: all are essential. Needless to say the secretary should be on the phone, be good at organising, and be ready to pick up any jobs without an obvious home.

The stewards

Even the most contented of communities will have their occasional moments of discord. A member may feel the system account is too much in minus, the administrators may feel it is inappropriate for a certain entry to be included in the directory, or there could be words spoken over the quality of a service supplied.

Such rankles may seem important at the time and it can be useful for there to be a group of three stewards or mediators to conciliate and settle such disputes. The three should have no other role in the administration, and should have a general power to settle all disputes. Three is a useful number if they can't reach unanimous agreement.

The post-box

You can make it easy for members to communicate with the administrators by providing a post-box for cheques, membership applications etc. at a central point in the town or shopping centre. Often a friendly shopkeeper will help. Stroud, Malvern, Totnes and Leamington Lets all have post-boxes at cafés in town centres where people can leave envelopes.

Calderdale has gone one better: there are post-boxes in every library for members to use. These boxes should be secure because although most of the mail will be Lets cheques, some will include subscriptions.

Stationery

Like virtually everything else, Lets needs its red tape. To run Lets you will need:

- An application form with space for names, address and phone numbers, and offers and wants. The form should also include the members' agreement (see the Appendix), a description of how the system works, and space to record when the subscription was paid.
- A welcome letter for new members reminding them how to trade, thanking them for their subscription, and if possible giving the deadline for the next directory.
- Chequebooks for the members.
- Reminders that subscriptions are due.
- The directory.
- Covering letter to be mailed with the directory.
- Letter to be sent periodically reminding members that they

Cheques issued by Manchester Lets (top) and The Wye Exchange, Hereford (below). The former can be printed in bulk, the latter are numbered and named.

should update their directory entries and telling them that either they will be repeated unchanged, or they will be deleted.

The subscription and membership

Any payments made to the administrators come from the members and the amount collected needs to be roughly equivalent to how much in Lets units it costs to compile the directory and maintain the accounts. These units can be collected in a variety of ways.

- You can charge a flat Lets fee per month or per year. This has the advantage of allowing the administrators to know exactly what their income is. But a flat fee bears no relationship to how much trading a member does, so the frequent trader, in effect, is subsidised by the infrequent trader. This may not be a disadvantage since you want to encourage people to trade and charging them even if they don't can persuade them to do so!

- You can levy a percentage charge on the sum changing hands. This method may mean your accountant has to deal with small fractions of Lets units, and it penalises members making few transactions of high volume.

- Yet another alternative is to charge a flat fee on each transaction. Manchester charges six Bobbins every two months and pays its administrators six Bobbins per hour (the Bobbin is valued at £1 by the system but some members ignore this). Malvern charges six Beacons for a book of ten cheques (four Beacons is roughly worth an hour of basic work) and pays its administrators four Beacons per hour.

Don't charge too much. Lets groups are springing up throughout the country and if your subscription rates are high, you may find another system in your town snapping at your heels with a lower subscription charge. And to add insult to injury, it may not be non-profit making Lets, but a commercial bartering company with the aim of making profits for its founder.

Annual subscriptions

You may want to consider whether annual subscriptions are needed at all. The problem with subscriptions is that after a year a demand arrives on the doormat, and the first impulse is to look at it later... The second impulse may be to reflect that you've done little trading and so there's no reason to renew. The third impulse is to weave a route to the wastepaper basket or recycling pile.

Lets doesn't actually need people to renew: it needs a certain sum in sterling to pay the running costs. Stroud hopes to meet all its sterling costs through events, so in the future they won't need to ask members to renew.

One system does not strike members off when they don't renew: they keep them on the list but do not do anything for the member which might cost sterling. So the directory entries remain, and the cheques are processed, but nothing is sent to them. This is an effective way of keeping members who couldn't afford the sterling subscription. But it can only work if a small percentage of members are in this category, and the administrators deliberately don't even advertise this service on their literature for fear that too many people take advantage of the arrangement.

Membership support

New — and old — members can find it valuable to have a person in the management group who can give them advice. Such a person is particularly valuable for helping tease out people's skills and wants which may not be at the forefront of their minds, or which they don't realise someone else might need or offer.

You can take this job further so the person actually arranges trades — a sort of broker. This will increase the workload (and the telephone bills) and it remains to be seen if it is justified by the extra trading that results. However it needs to be said that non-Lets commercial bartering networks (see Chapter 9) rely on full-time brokers to facilitate most of their transactions so they presumably find it useful.

It is best to avoid developing systems of quality control. One system tried rating members' abilities to perform the services they offered. Don't. Ask yourself: how do you decide objectively and fairly how good a person is at their job? And how much time would it take to make these assessments of members?

The decision on whether to trade should be taken solely by the buyer and the seller: the administrators shouldn't seek to influence it. The administrator can give a prospective buyer the names of other members who have recently traded with a particular person, and the hopeful buyer can then consult the previous customers for 'references'. If you go further than that you'll probably find trouble. The time is not yet ripe for a Lets version of *Which?* magazine!

This chapter has addressed the basic requirements for keeping Lets running. But since systems are always striving for something better, many have developed initiatives to boost trading and help them on the road to success.

If your system is short of competent people, concentrate on these bare necessities of life. If you are able to put some legwork in to expand the system, there are many bright ideas for you to follow and try out. Some of these are discussed in the next chapter.

CHAPTER 7

Keeping your system running smoothly

A marvellous, marvellous idea.
It may sound strange. What is
important is that it works.
WOMAN'S OWN

C reating your own trading relationships in a community of
Lets members is a very new experience for all of us. Until
the arrival of Lets in the UK in the late 1980s few of us
could conceive that we could join an instant community and buy
and sell without pounds changing hands.

Hence signing up to Lets is just the first step for most
members: they will need to be drawn in to the way it works.
Many will need gentle coaxing to get them to phone a stranger
and ask for some work to be done. They will need to be told again
and again that it really is all right to spend, spend, spend. They
are also likely to need some persuading that other members' skills
really are professional.

So your system is likely to benefit from a few bright ideas that
bring people together and stimulate trade. The picture emerging
is that it takes a little while before most people dive right into the
water: in the early months of membership they are likely just to
dip a toe in and do one or two small trades. Then as they meet
more people and come to know them, they will feel more confident, and trading will increase.

One of the biggest problems is leading members on from
merely making *occasional* purchases on Lets to making *regular*

purchases. This is very important, for in the early days of membership it is easy to forget that a job could be done on Lets. One Malvern member confided that when she needed some windows repaired, she rang up someone in the phone book and only realised afterwards that she could have got it done on Lets. Once she had become fully aware of the possibilities, she has been busily trading ever since. Moving people from the occasional to the regular trade means they get the habit of using Lets — in the way we already have the habit of using cash.

Markets, trading days and socials

Experience shows that members are more keen to trade when they know others personally. Indeed many members are finding that a major benefit is meeting people, with the actual trading being a secondary consideration.

Social events and markets are an effective way of helping people to meet one another and increase their trading. New members particularly are prompted to begin trading having met some of the other members at an event.

The events need not be designed primarily for trading or for socialising. Many members will aim to socialise *and* trade at a Lets event. Indeed an event billed as a social allows members to informally and discreetly assess whether they want to trade with someone.

It's best to keep the administration of these events outside the system account and run them as stand alone operations.

In the early days of the system, trading days when people can put faces to names can be very useful. Goods for sale or hire can be displayed, and members can be given space on noticeboards to list wants and offers. Costs such as for hiring the hall can be covered by those charging those attending in sterling, and charging Lets to cover the organiser's time.

In Malvern the Tea & Trading Days allow people to sip tea and munch cakes while looking at goods and services for sale. In Newbury they organise regular get togethers in a local hall with music supplied by a band paid in Lets. Other ideas there have included ghost story evenings, and sing-songs around the piano. Stroud has a good line in gigs in a community hall.

But don't forget: these events can be organised differently from the way other organisations arrange such get-togethers:

- try to find a room or a hall which you can hire for Lets;
- charge members in Lets for having a stall or perhaps in the form of a percentage of transactions;
- charge for food in Lets;
- pay the cooks in Lets (a small sterling charge to eaters should cover the cost of ingredients);
- pay the person who arranges the day in Lets;
- put up noticeboards for people to write up services offered and wanted; and
- make sure you have a stall where people can find out how Lets works and — most importantly — can join.

This is also the opportunity to use some gentle financial inducements to persuade people to join.

Say you charge members three Lets units plus £1 for entrance to an evening including dinner (where the unit is equivalent to the pound) and £4 for non-members. Tell non-members they can join Lets on the door, and pay the entrance fee as a member. In Newbury non-members are charged even more in sterling, with the option that the ticket cost goes towards their subscription if they decide to join.

Val Oldaker, one of the administrators of Newbury Lets, seeks out members with high minus balances and suggests they arrange the socials so they can earn Lets from doing the organising.

THE TOTNES TRADING POST

Every week in a Totnes hall, the tables groan with a mixture of foods and produce made by Lets members. All are available for Acorns, and the 'trading post' (as it is called) is held in the centre of town on market day.

The event was started by a member, Ruth Zimmerman, as a way of allowing members to sell food on a regular basis and it has rapidly established itself as the place to buy wholesome home-made food as part of the weekly shopping trip.

The sterling costs of the project (mainly paying for the

hall) are met by a wise tie-up with a local commercial vegetable grower. The grower sells boxes of vegetables (for pounds) as part of a Community Supported Agriculture scheme. Under this scheme customers agree to buy a box of vegetables each week, the exact mix of vegetables being dependent on the season: the customer agrees to take 'pot-luck'. The CSA scheme needed a drop-off point in town for customers to collect the boxes, and they supply a free box to Ruth who sells it for pounds to pay for the hall. The Lets trading rides on the back of this deal which also brings in people collecting their vegetables.

Ruth runs the market with help from a couple of other members, so the people making the food can merely drop off their wares before the market opens and collect anything unsold at the end of the day — they don't need to be present the whole time. After four months, the market was turning over nearly 200 units each week in a varying mix of pounds and Acorns.

The project was pump-primed by the Lets system account which granted 350 Acorns to Ruth to pay those running the market.

'The customers are running ahead of the suppliers,' says Ruth. 'We are swept clear in just over three hours.'

Sellers charge in a mix of Acorns or pounds as they want, and Ruth maintains a transactions sheet where buyers sign for the Lets element of what they are buying and the sheet shows what has been sold and who has earned what. At the end of the day she gives a statement to the Lets accounts administrator who brings members' accounts up to date.

Ruth is adamant that she is not running a shop: she says that shops are predictable places with predictable stocks. In the trading post there is an ever changing range of goods. People are encouraged to join Lets as they see the quality of food they can buy once they are members.

And the lesson that demand outstrips supply is especially significant since Totnes is a town of high unemployment...

Extending the skills on offer

One of the sadder features of modern life is the number of people who believe they have nothing that people would want to buy from them on Lets. They're saying, in effect, that they have no time, no skills, no experience, no possessions, and no knowledge which could be of use to their friends and neighbours.

However, one of the lessons most people learn from Lets is that we all have something to contribute. Just because we can't sell our skills to a large employer on an industrial estate or afford to invest in expensive technology to practise them, it doesn't mean we can't offer useful services to our neighbours.

In Appendix 1 there is an Inspiration List showing many of the trades which have been offered nationwide on Lets. This list can be supplemented by nominating an imaginative member as adviser. The adviser's job is just that: s/he talks with members (especially new ones) and draws out the skills they can offer. Because many of us are not used to broad thinking about our skills, we imagine that many of the things we do are simply of no interest to others.

Targeting potential members

Lets groups are open to all people, whatever their walk of life, skills or experience. But some members are likely to be in greater demand than others. Experience shows that the services most needed are of the basic household type — decorating, painting, plumbing, clearing drains, electrics, babysitting, car repairs etc.

Thus it would be reasonable for systems to set out deliberately to attract members with these skills.

Talking to the relevant trade associations can spread the message, as can encouraging people with contacts in these jobs to bring their friends along.

Remind much needed plumbers and electricians that it's fine for them to charge a proportion in Lets, and the rest in pounds. This can help alleviate the fear that they will suddenly find themselves with more Lets units than they can readily spend and with a reducing sterling income (a position a skilled worker can easily get into). They can also vary the proportions over time according to how much of each they need. You can also attract such people by, at the same time, finding members offering items such as food so the other 'blue collar' workers see they can save sterling by joining.

Attracting new members and keeping old ones

There are several arrangements for attracting and keeping members.

- Joint members at the same address can be charged the same as a single member. The system's only extra work is additional directory entries which you want to encourage. There is no extra work involved in running joint accounts.

- Half-yearly subscriptions are a useful facility for those unemployed or on income support. For while £8 a year may be a small sum for those in full-time work, for those with little money it can be a large sum for membership of something that is new and in which they may not yet have full confidence.

- It is also helpful to charge a lower concessionary rate.

Increasing the trading

Trading can be encouraged by offering discounts on transaction charges to people trading in their first month or two of membership. Similar discounts could be introduced, say, in the depths of winter, when activity tends to slow down.

Alternatively you could try levying a 'non-trading charge' on people who neither buy nor sell so as to encourage them to trade. But think carefully about this as it can discourage people who are nervous at going into what they see as debt, or it can encourage a member who may have been ill and unable to trade to leave altogether.

Using the asterisk

The asterisk can be a very useful tool in your directory or newsletter. While it is not necessarily good practice for the directory to become an advertising sheet, there is no reason why

Manchester LETS
Social/Trading Event

SATURDAY MARCH 26th
6:30pm to 9:30pm
Friends Meeting House, Mount St

Bring goods and skills to trade
Ask questions or make suggestions
You can join on the day

Help needed with:
Setting up and clearing away
Greetings table and Info desk
Refreshment stall (please bring donations)
Car parking and helping disabled
Q & A Sessions

The flyer for an event run by Manchester Lets. The advertisement shrewdly mixes the social and trading elements of Lets.

members shouldn't be able to see who on the list particularly wants to trade. For example, new members often feel they want to do some selling before they buy: so flagging them with an asterisk can encourage others to make a point of giving them their business.

An asterisk next to a member wanting to address a high minus balance can signal that they also particularly want to earn some Lets.

Shops and noticeboards

Many systems have arranged for noticeboards to be installed in shops, cafés or libraries. Such boards operate on the same principle as the private advertisements in newsagents' windows — except that the ads are for goods and services in Lets.

Such boards have the advantage of allowing short-life advertisements when the publication date of the next directory is still some time away.

In Calderdale where the post-boxes are in the libraries, Lets details are also to be found on the libraries' own computer information system with screens available for access by all library users.

Using the wants columns

The wants section in the directory is as important as the offers, so don't see it as the poor relation. In our advertising-driven economy we are used to being barraged with invitations to buy. We are not so used to seeing announcements of what people *want*. Seeing other people's wants can persuade members to widen the scope of what they do, and can allow them to make an occasional trade. For instance a member may not wish to advertise house moving help because they don't want to be in frequent demand for shifting pianos. But they may be prepared to help a particular person advertising for such help. They may also be prepared to experiment and try doing something they haven't done before — and responding to another member's want advert can prompt new ideas.

The wants column can also be used to attract new members, as Newbury Lets found. A member seeing that a particular service is wanted can use this announcement to persuade a friend who could do the job to join.

The local press

Commercial local newspapers often don't charge for advertisements for goods under a certain price, often £10. Members could use these for advertising services in Lets. Similarly areas which have community newspapers may be open to members advertising goods for Lets.

The 100 club

Glanford Lets in Humberside runs a 100 club. These clubs work by members subscribing a certain amount in Lets per month which entitles them to take part in a regular draw with more Lets units as the prize.

You don't even need to collect the fees as you do in a conventional 100 club — the payment is just deducted from the accounts. But make sure the other members know who the winners are and keep up a sense of excitement.

However, caution is needed with 100 clubs: see Chapter 11 for information on the legal position.

Giving Lets

You can also introduce a Lets gift voucher which is redeemable with any member. The voucher can be an unusual gift and may be instrumental in introducing a new member to the system. If you do decide to operate a voucher system, decide whether to allow them to be given to non-members, and, if so, whether temporary memberships need to be granted to such people to enable them to receive a directory and write cheques.

Donations to charities and other organisations

There is no reason why members shouldn't give Lets donations to organisations whose work they support. Such an arrangement allows a person who has little money to give some help to a charity. In Hereford a day centre for people with disabilities would welcome donations of Lets so they can pay people to take their users for outings.

Donations can be given to a charity *whether or not* the recipient is already a Lets member. If the charity is not a member, the donation could be used to persuade the organisation to join. Or the donating member could buy goods and services direct which would go to the organisation.

Pruning

When a Lets network grows larger and has been running for a couple of years, it may build up a quantity of what we could loosely term 'dead wood'. These are account holders who have moved or lost interest, or whose circumstances have changed and who feel unable to participate, or who have died.

While their offers in the directory may give the impression of a wide range of services available, in actual practice their announcements mean other members keep making fruitless phone calls before finding someone willing to do a job.

This is the time to prune. Totnes and Stroud have been doing this, and the process involves sending notices to all members asking them to confirm that they are still available to trade.

In Stroud, the administrators did their pruning entirely separately from when the subscriptions were due, and although 100 members didn't reply to the circular, 80 of these were encouraged to remain members after being chased up by phone. Many of these 80 welcomed the phone call from the administrators as a chance to settle a small problem about Lets.

The likelihood is that the system will lose some members, but you will weed out those who have gone away, and hence provide a better service for the members who are still busily trading.

CHAPTER 8

When debt is a good thing

*One should never wait until
you see money running along
in front so you may follow. It is
you who leads, and money
follows.*

F. FRASER DARLING

The bailiffs, the bankruptcy court, high interest rates, the loan shark, the bank manager's letter, houseowners' negative equity, red bills, even the debtors' prison. No wonder the average Lets member is reluctant to go into debt.

Yet it is the failure to address or understand the issue of debt that is probably the biggest single obstacle to Lets becoming a mainstay of the community.

Because we are a society where for most people cash is in limited supply, the blackguard who spends merrily on Lets and then does a runner is seen as the rogue who will bring the whole edifice tumbling down. Indeed the question, 'What's to stop someone just spending and then disappearing?' is the one most often asked by people new to Lets.

The question is a product of the economy we live in: we are encouraged to acquire as much of that scarce resource — money — as we can, and use it to buy as many possessions as possible with not a thought for the people we are buying from. It is also an economy where we trust each other less and less: how many shopkeepers now accept cheques without a guarantee card?

Why it is essential to spend, spend, spend.

The Lets economy, however, is very different. Think of it in miniature: if six friends form their own system, list the services they are offering and only start trading when they have Lets units in hand to spend, what happens? As we saw in Chapter 5, the answer is quite simple: nothing. There will be no trading because none of them has any Lets units to spend.

The system only starts operating when one member hires another for some work or buys goods from them, and writes them out a Lets cheque which shows up in the accounts as one plus and one minus transaction. The wealth of that Lets community (or the size of its economy if you like) is shown by the number of Lets units which have been created by the trading. As more of the six create Lets units by spending them, so the Lets economy grows.

The crucial point is that creating the Lets units like this is not going into debt. It is not comparable with sterling where someone has to lend you the cash (leaving them the poorer until you pay them back), nor do you have to pay any interest, or pay the money back by a certain date. By earning Lets you do not deprive anyone else.

When members create Lets units they are entering into a *commitment* to do some work at some time in future for someone in the system. *That is all they are doing.* There is no meaningful comparison with borrowing money from a bank.

If a friend said they would give you a lift to the hospital in return for you helping out another friend at another time you would hardly give it a thought. You'd part at the hospital with the words: 'I'll owe you one'.

That is all you are doing on Lets. You are saying to the community of Lets members: 'I owe you one. When someone else asks me to do something I will do it if I possibly can.'

Some people say that Lets runs on trust: it does, but it is not necessary for people in Lets to trust each other when they join. For the system *builds up the necessary trust,* and as people trade their trust in each other increases.

It is the *buyer* much more than the seller who dictates how Lets will grow since it is the buyer who is the main influence on whether a trade takes place. It is far easier for a buyer to find a seller than it is for a seller to seek out a buyer, even on Lets. So the buyers carry a heavy responsibility: they are the engine which drives the Lets economy. They have the potential to take Lets out of the ghetto so it can meet many more of people's needs. There's a social duty on the members to buy and thereby enter into a commitment to do some work on the system.

Indeed, according to John Rhodes, one of the founders of Stroud Lets, a person with a high minus is of more potential use to the community than someone with a high plus. For the community can call on the person with a minus to do some work, whereas the community itself will have to do some work for the person with a high plus balance. Lets is a whole new way of looking at money.

HEY BIG SPENDER!

According to Val Oldaker, one of the Newbury Lets administrators, their breakthrough in trading came when member Jim Wallis earned 1500 New Berries for 75 hours of work repairing a car.

'He had so many New Berries, he just started spending,' said Val. 'It was a sea change with everyone having a completely new mindset. He bought a waistcoat and had some interior design advice, and paid some rent for where his van was parked. He had his jumper darned and bought some cooked food. He had all those New Berries but no money and said he needed food so people fed him! It stimulated the whole system.'

The result, according to Val, was that as people earned Lets they felt more confident about spending — and felt more confident about creating even more. And the person who hired Jim is now slowly meeting the commitment he entered into — and is happily driving about in his old car.

It follows that members who earn large amounts of Lets units but don't spend them are not being as community-minded as they might think. They may be doing a lot of work for people in their community, but they aren't helping other members to reduce their minus balances. The system needs those units to continue circulating. A member in deep credit is not wholly an asset to the system.

This message about debt has to be explained very clearly to members. It is a message which should appear in the directory and on the accounts statements, on the application forms and in the newsletters, on the noticeboards and in the local newspaper. You also need to explain it to any journalists you talk to.

What if someone does a runner?

The fear that a member may build up a large minus balance and then abscond is a subject which exercises people new to the Lets concept.

What does indeed happen if a member departs having done a lot of spending? This question can't be answered in one sentence: there are several characteristics of the Lets design which make it unlikely that people spend and then disappear, and also ensure that neither the system nor the members suffer if they do.

The history of Lets in the UK so far is that people don't join to abuse it: there are hardly any cases of people who have joined, spent extensively, and then quit. There are some cases where administrators are watching particular accounts rather carefully, but none have needed any action apart from some quiet advice.

The reason this abuse does not take place is because most economic crime in our society is against strangers and anonymous institutions. Lets networks are, in contrast, communities of people: not everyone will know one other, but they will know where people live and may know something about them.

The Lets accounts are available for all members to see, so a high spender will be very visible. High spenders who do little or no work in return know that other members will see the scale of their spending and they will have to face the resulting social embarrassment. Furthermore other members are likely to know not only that the person is a high spender but also that they have been refusing to take on any Lets work offered — and it is here that the abuse can be detected. A member with a high minus balance who is widening the range of services offered and taking on any jobs they are given will be seen in a different light from a member busily spending and refusing to take work.

It is also likely that a person who is known to be spending without having the commitment to give to the system may find other members unwilling to sell to them.

It is these features which allow the administrators to keep a discreet eye on such accounts. They will know that particular members have built up a high minus balance because they have just moved house and are still busy getting it straight. Or that others have just had a baby and are buying clothes, pushchairs and other accoutrements but will start doing some work in a few months' time.

YOU HAVE TO WIDEN YOUR SCOPE

Manchester has a member who should be every system's favourite: she is continually creating Lets by spending, and continually earning it back by using imagination and flair to dream up new sources of income. She does, however, have a bedrock of Lets income through running the office administration, but says this regular income is not the prime reason why she has the confidence to spend.

She is a single parent on a low cash income. Since being on Lets she has had her kitchen redecorated, shelves put up, lifts provided, a henhouse built, fencing erected, and sacks of firewood delivered.

'I don't even look at my account,' she says, 'I'm probably hundreds of Bobbins in the red, but I don't care. There used to be a community living here where people knew each other and could knock on each others' door for help. You can't do that now. But the Bobbin breaks the barrier. It is fine for people to spend and spend as long as they are prepared to do things back. And on Lets people do the things they enjoy doing!'

She is horrified that anyone could imagine that such an attitude to going into 'debt' on Lets indicates she has a cavalier approach to handling pounds: 'I certainly don't do the same thing with sterling,' she says, 'I have an absolute dread of going into debt there. When I joined Lets I had the same dread, but I became convinced that I don't need to earn before I spend as long as at some time in the future I balance my account. I don't see it as going into debt: I see it as committing myself to doing things for other members. But you have to be versatile in what you offer, and you have to widen your scope.'

If the administrators are concerned about an account, they can help the person to develop some new offers, or (with his or her agreement) can mark their entry in the directory with an asterisk to encourage people to buy from them.

A system may agree to set a maximum limit that any one member is allowed to go into minus. Some systems have erred on the side of caution and done this and it may have set members' minds at rest, but it shouldn't really be necessary in the early days. When networks grow larger with many thousands of people involved the situation may change.

The ultimate answer to someone who takes advantage is quite simple: the administrators can strike the person's name off the system. This is a world away from a person going bankrupt, for the people to whom they have written Lets cheques *still have those Lets credited to their accounts.* The cheques don't bounce, so no individual loses. It can be said that the community as a whole loses if a person departs leaving a high minus, but as long as it is a small proportion of the system's total turnover it is very unlikely to affect members' trading.

This is an important difference from the world of sterling. For sterling is a scarce resource: if one person spends more than they can repay, someone else has to lose. Lets is not scarce: it is created at will by the members going into commitment with each other.

In practice, on Lets, people leaving with minus balances seem to equal those leaving with plus balances.

And with all the policing in the world, what are you going to do about the member who dies with a minus balance? Will they be pursued to Another Place so they can bring their account back to zero? Or will Lets units have to figure in members' wills?

THE BANKRUPT MEMBER

An undischarged bankrupt who went bust with debts of £76,000 and who has run up a £2500 Lets commitment may not seem every system's ideal member. But John Rhodes says he has only had one person commenting to him about the 2500 Strouds he is in commitment.

John was one of Stroud Lets' founder members and in four years estimates that he has done over £8000 worth of trading on his personal Lets account, and a further £7000 on his business accounts. He is fully committed to the system and his businesses are often called upon to provide landscaping and tree care services for members. In turn he spends Strouds employing casual labour and has bought many Strouds' worth of osteopathy after he seriously injured his back falling out of a tree.

```
MALVERN LETS BARTER - A SUMMARY OF MEMBER TRANSACTIONS

Up to 20.03.94 (All members' balances initially zero)
```

	Credits	Debits	Balance
Lets Barter	220.00	295.00	-75.00
Penn A	0.00	4.00	-4.00
Pickering G. Newsome E.	212.00	102.00	110.00
Parry H	26.00	8.00	18.00
Morgan O	78.00	23.00	55.00
Seymour Y	4.00	10.00	-6.00
Shaw V	172.00	22.00	150.00
Brown R. Sewell H	29.00	36.50	-7.50
Pullen S	00.00	15.00	-15.00
Towers G	60.00	52.50	7.50
Jones G	00.00	151.00	-151.00

Some of the accounts of the Malvern system. Malvern sends out the accounts of all members when the trading levels indicate sizeable changes to accounts - perhaps three times a year. Actual names are used in the statements, but false names have been used here to protect members' privacy.

'If I hadn't been in Lets I would have been in real trouble after the accident,' he says. 'I had to get a lot of medical help and support like having meals cooked for me, shopping fetched and getting the house cleaned. Lets provided an effective support system and it was nice because I had never had that sort of support since I was eight years old.' The illness and John's attitude that Lets will only succeed if people create the credits by spending them, led him into having a high turnover as well as a high commitment. The Lets income from his landscaping

---

Manchester LETS Balance and Turnover Figures at 31.01.94

LETS is an open community system. Any member is entitled to know the balance and turnover of another member's account. The Core Group will also publish these details from time to time. To save printing costs, this list only shows those accounts with a turnover (Ins plus Outs) of at least 75 Bobbins.

Name	Ins	Outs	Balance
George Smit	146.00	16.10	129.90
Freda Maxwell	49.00	26.00	23.00
Sue Leighton	84.00	52.10	31.90
Caroline Johnson	159.00	121.00	38.00
Jo Bransom	84.00	47.00	37.00
Susanna Peret	152.60	187.00	−34.40
Deborah Robinson	71.00	35.20	35.80
Fred Jones	00.00	112.00	−112.00
Mark Leigh	181.00	129.00	52.00
Bernard Drew	113.00	102.30	10.70
Dawn Dewar	20.00	66.00	−46.00
Chris McCarthy	96.00	91.00	5.00
David and Lyn Lawe	00.00	118.00	−118.00
Mark Par	43.00	163.00	−120.00
Mike Phipps	109.00	69.00	40.00

A snapshot of some of the accounts of the much larger Manchester system. The full list of all accounts where more than 75 Bobbins have been traded is printed in the newsletters which go to all members. Real names are used in the newsletter, but in this extract we have used false names to protect members' privacy.

"WELL MR SIMPSON
HOW CAN WE HELP YOU
ADDRESS YOUR MINUS?

LETS
ADMINISTRATOR

business meant he could be fairly confident of getting
enough work to meet the Lets commitment.

But his affairs in the world of sterling were going quite
differently. At one point he had loans from 13 finance
houses and the local council totalling nearly £140,000.
Although the interest rate for some of it was as high as 38
per cent the business was producing sufficient income to
service the debt. He was repaying £1200 a month until a
customer defaulted on a deal, leaving him high and dry
with expensive equipment lying idle.

'We extended the payback period, and halved the
repayments, but we had no money to live on,' says John.
Then as the business slowly recovered he paid back most
of the local people and shops who had lent him money,
and then went bankrupt.

'To set up a business you have to borrow money, and
if you don't have it yourself you have to go to finance
houses where smart suited people sit in offices and get
very rich from the high interest they charge you,' he says.

'It is impossible to get a business right the first time, and you have to deal with other companies which don't pay their bills on time, or who don't pay at all because they know you don't have the money to sue. As the interest mounts you can be stuck with that debt for years and years. But all the finance houses say is that if you don't pay back by a certain time, they will take away your house. It's outrageous. Most of the people who go bankrupt do so because something went wrong that was beyond their ability to control.

'Lets however, is there to help people in the community. Lets works in an honourable way so I will work in an honourable way with them, and will pay back my commitment. Lets is not holding me by the balls and saying they'll have interest on every penny!'

Changing the language of debt

The government learnt the lesson many years ago that changing the words can change the message. In years past UK politicians changed the name of the Ministry of War to the Ministry of Defence, and the nuclear centre Windscale which had acquired a sinister reputation became Sellafield (which has since inherited the same sinister reputation).

In the world of Lets, members are ceasing to talk about 'debt'. A minus balance is not a debt. Some describe it as being 'in commitment' which sums up the position nicely.

A private agreement to buy

An effective way of persuading people that it really is all right to spend before they've earned is to show them examples of people doing just that. The administrators of some systems have decided that they will personally undertake to go heavily into commitment with the dual aim of giving credits to new members and those as yet reluctant to buy, and to be able to show on the accounts that some members are busily spending — and they are not being cold-shouldered by the rest of the community.

The administrators can do this because they — of all the members — are likely to be seen as committed to the system, and not the sort of people likely to be abusing it.

Giving everyone Lets

So since a common problem for members is the fear of going into debt, why not give everyone on the system, say, 100 Lets units so their accounts start at +100 rather than zero?

The idea is attractive at first sight, and several systems have adopted this process, including Abingdon and Haverfordwest. Malvern has given Lets to people who bring in new members. Letting people think they have Lets units ready to spend is an effective psychological ploy.

But, where do these Lets come from? Perhaps it doesn't matter, because all that happens is that the transactions will not add up to zero. Perhaps they come from the system account which is supposed to finance administration. Perhaps the administrators set up an account for the purpose which always shows a hefty minus. All these permutations are possible, but all may have the same effect of undermining confidence in the Lets unit.

In a small system where members know each other, it is unlikely to make much difference if these accounts are showing deficits — everyone knows that the Lets units are just being played with to make members more comfortable when spending. But while systems are still breaking into the mainstream they need to build up confidence among the general public who are likely to perceive a heavy minus balance, or figures which don't add up, as signs of poor administration. And an impression of poor administration is something to be avoided when you are trying to build up confidence in the system.

Furthermore you may just end up with your members having no proper understanding about why it is good for them to be in commitment. So instead of being reluctant to have a minus figure in their account, they may just be reluctant to have a figure of less than +100 recorded.

So if you are planning to dispense Lets to all members to put them in immediate credit, think the issues through very carefully and be aware that you may be making a rod to beat your back with in years to come.

Accounting for the departed

The theory of Lets is that all the balances should add up to zero. But when a member departs with a plus or minus balance this amount needs to 'go' somewhere for accounting purposes. If it is simply deleted from the system, the accounts won't add up to zero ever again.

The best practice is to move these balances to an inactive members' account, so the amounts still figure in the system (and can be reclaimed if a departed member is readmitted), but are not included in the month by month statements of trading.

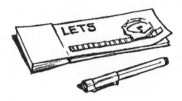

CHAPTER 9

Let's do business

It is easier to make money with paper chasing paper than by investing in real goods and services.

PAUL VOLKER,
US FEDERAL RESERVE

In the boom and bust economy, businesses suffer when customer numbers decline. Staff morale drops off as employees don't know whether they will keep their jobs, and interest rates on loans remain high.

The irony is that businesses which have traded enthusiastically in Lets have found that this part of their turnover is immune to these problems. The most eager business to trade in Lets has found it is earning too much, and it needs to keep its Lets income in control.

Another business is in debit to the equivalent of £6000 — yet it is not paying any interest, and it does not receive irate letters from the Lets administrators asking when it is to be paid back.

For many businesses such a financial position would be like a dream come true. Yet, although there are still difficulties for businesses trading in Lets, these early indications show the considerable potential Lets has for helping shops and factories with their trading. Indeed the difficulties are, in the main, only present because these are still early days for Lets, and as the systems become larger, businesses will find it easier to trade.

The evidence is that since Lets units are not scarce, the recession and resulting reluctance to spend sterling will not apply to Lets buyers, and business will improve.

They will not only be able to attract custom that will not go to their non-Lets competitors, but they will also eventually *receive back the Lets units they spend,* for Lets units generally stay within the local economy.

The majority of trading carried out in modern societies is through businesses. Thus if Lets members want their system to take its place in providing many of people's everyday needs and wants, then businesses need to be attracted to join.

If, on the other hand, the members' prime interest is to stimulate contact between individuals, the system need do no more than accept businesses applying to join, but not seek them out.

It must be remembered however, that as businesses do join, so more individual members will join as they are attracted by the opportunity to buy from (and sell to) those businesses.

The advantages to a business

By joining, a business will help itself by attracting increased custom, and at the same time assist the local economy. This applies whether or not the business is locally owned, for the Lets units the business earns can generally only be spent within the local system.

The advantages to businesses include:

- a higher sterling income when customers who might not have bought at all pay for products in part-cash and part-Lets.
- free advertising;
- an increase in their customer base beyond those who are sterling rich to include those who are sterling-poor but can earn Lets;
- reductions in their sterling outlays as they buy in stock or labour from local people who can charge in Lets units, or where the owner takes out or pays some wages in Lets;
- an improved local reputation as they are seen to have a commitment to the local economy.

To gain these benefits, a business owner will need to keep a careful eye on how the company participates in the system.

Businesses will find the benefits increase gradually over time and different types of business will have different experiences. In the early days of a system, labour intensive businesses will be able to benefit most, but as the systems become bigger, shops for whom stock is a major overhead will be able to buy more goods on Lets.

Most companies will probably want to begin by charging for goods in a mix of sterling and Lets. The proportions can be varied from time to time according to the opportunities for spending the Lets credits. Sterling has had hundreds of years to become established and there are no shortages of opportunities for spending pounds. Lets units have only been around for a few short years, and in a new system with a small membership it is likely to take time before there are opportunities to spend large sums in Lets. But businesses should not be disheartened if at first they are finding it easier to earn than to spend Lets — each shop or café joining acts as a spur to persuade other people to join, and this in turn encourages suppliers to be prepared to sell to the businesses for Lets.

Administrators wanting to attract businesses into a system could offer to let them join and spend for six months with no requirement to sell. This would allow a business to buy on the system 'without obligation' and thus see that there are real opportunities for using any Lets credits they earn.

Business owners would be advised to run a separate personal Lets account so it is clear to the Inland Revenue which earnings and spending are work related, and which are personal. (See Chapter 11 for more details on the tax position.)

It may be best for administrators to advise limited companies that the Lets commitment must be guaranteed by the directors personally (as bank loans often are), so if the company goes into liquidation, the directors can't walk away from the Lets commitment as they would from most of their sterling liabilities.

Businesses planning to employ people for Lets should be cautious. Paying one-off freelance fees in Lets makes the recipient liable for tax if he or she is in a high enough earnings bracket. But when an employee's wages are above £56 per week — even when paid in Lets — there are additional complications such as national insurance contributions.

Shops which are selling a multitude of small products may

find it easier to have a 'slate' for Lets members to sign when purchasing, rather than demanding a separate cheque for each transaction. As the systems grow larger, shopkeepers would need to satisfy themselves that an unknown buyer is indeed a Lets member.

On the book-keeping side, all that is needed are additional columns in the main accounts for Lets income and outgoings.

Safeguarding the interests of businesses

Businesses will also want to be assured that, at least in the early life of a system, they are not substantially losing sterling income by receiving Lets units instead.

There are a variety of ways of dealing with this issue:

- they can offer goods at a proportion of Lets to customers who spend at least a certain amount over a given period. So a person could buy goods at, say, 40 per cent Lets after they've spent £50 during a single month. This would encourage 'customer loyalty' (an attribute Lets naturally encourages), and would also mean the shopkeeper could keep some control in the early stages to make sure they don't lose sterling income.

- the shop could only offer for sale the goods they are able to buy for Lets. Thus a greengrocer could accept Lets credits for vegetables they buy from a member, while other goods are sold for sterling. A stationer could sell greetings cards printed by a Lets member, or a member could supply cakes on Lets to a baker's shop.

- a business could expand its range because of its Lets involvement. A shop selling new books could buy and sell some secondhand books on Lets: this could bring additional customers into the shop who might not otherwise visit.

- since Lets is effective at promoting labour intensive work such as repairs, a shop could offer this service for Lets as an expansion of its normal business of selling products.

- the business owners could persuade their local suppliers to join. This would be a better contribution to Lets, and could help a local supplier who would then themselves gain the benefits of Lets membership.

EXPLAINING LETS

Explaining Lets to the local business community is particularly important. One system needed to improve its contacts as this letter from the Vice Chair of Exmouth Chamber of Commerce shows:

"The Lets proposal, on the face of it, appears to be encouraging the very type of trading that undermines the businesses of our members. Carried to its ultimate conclusion, non-commercial trading of this type can seriously damage, or even cause the collapse of, a local economy and bring about the failure of legitimate businesses. Ad hoc 'jobbing' of the type envisaged is generally carried out by individuals who do not carry business overheads such as provision of premises with appropriate insurances, rents, and business rates; and very often the other on-costs required of a bona-fide trader to comply with requirements for health and safety, fire regulations and food hygiene laws, public liability insurances etc. are ignored. In consequence, the consumer is put at risk, and the legitimate business is unable to compete economically which can result in the laying-off of employees and a general increase in unemployment.

"The need for an alternative currency ('cockles' and 'mussels') seems very questionable indeed as the nation has a perfectly satisfactory trading medium in sterling. We can see no need or justification for change.

"What then is the benefit of the Lets scheme to its subscribers or the local economy? If the aim is to avoid taxation, or to enable a member to claim state benefits because he/she has little or no traditional finance or is without employment earning a taxable income, then we would see the scheme as most unethical. Perhaps you could clarify these points to us?

"Thank-you for your invitation to attend your official

opening on August 28, but our attendance would not seem entirely appropriate whilst we have doubts about the morality of the Lets scheme, and under the circumstances, we must decline to attend.

"Yours etc."

Maintaining confidence

Businesses particularly need to understand the issues surrounding minus balances and commitments. In the world of commerce, the death knell can sound for a business which is perceived as unable to pay its debts. Hence a high minus for a business may not be perceived by the owners as good advertising. The only solution is for the administrators to make it clear on statements that such minuses do not imply a poor reflection on the business — or any other member for that matter. The option of treating businesses differently from other members and not publishing their balances is not advisable since it is a cardinal principle of Lets that members should be able to know the extent of everyone's commitments.

The most successful Lets businesses

The UK business which has done the most trading in Lets units is Mills Café in Stroud.

Maggie Mills was one of the founders of Stroud Lets in 1990 and she joined her café up almost immediately. Since those early days Mills Café has turned over some 35,000 Strouds (the Stroud is more or less on a par with the pound).

Maggie admits that 'she couldn't foresee the consequences' when they started offering Lets members the opportunity to buy meals and drinks entirely in Strouds. 'I became involved because it struck me that Lets is a fantastic way of regenerating local economies, and I wanted to sort out the problems as they cropped up.

'We started out taking 100 per cent Strouds for all transactions and that worked okay for a little while,' she says. 'We were spending the Lets as we were taking them. This is the critical issue: if you can spend them they are just as good as sterling.'

The café now pays something over a quarter of its organic vegetable bill in Strouds, as well as the weekly bill for cleaning table cloths. A variety of odd jobs have been paid for with Lets in various proportions — the recent installation of a burglar alarm was charged at 50 per cent Strouds for the labour component. Other jobs paid partly in Lets have included rewiring the building and paying the company's accountant. Maggie and her co-owner have taken part of their wages in Strouds and have bought services and goods for themselves on the system.

The café now has a 6,000 Stroud credit which Maggie describes as manageable but she says she needs more ways to spend them before she will allow the figure to go higher.

She now varies the proportion of Lets to keep this figure in balance and does this by cutting the acceptance of Lets in the daytime — when the café is already busy — and accepting 25 or 50 per cent Lets in the evenings when there are fewer customers.

'We were aware we had one quiet evening and we offered to sell for 100 per cent Lets to give it a boost and sure enough we got really busy. People like to come to a busy place and we were taking Lets but we were also taking more sterling.'

Maggie admits the Lets income is not a high proportion of their total turnover. 'But offering 100 per cent Lets on Friday evenings did make a difference to our takings,' she says, 'and if we are taking 50 per cent Lets as we are now, we are still getting 50 per cent sterling on these transactions and we do get more people coming in. We get people in the evening who would not come if they had to pay entirely in sterling as they are Lets-rich and cash-poor.'

Maggie tried to use the extra Lets income to reward the staff by giving them a pay increase — the increase being in Strouds. The staff were willing, but then the Inland Revenue stepped in and insisted that the Lets component (as well as the pounds) was taxable and that the tax had to be paid in sterling. The result would have been that the staff received Strouds, but less sterling, as more pounds were deducted to pay the income tax and national insurance contribution.

At this point Maggie reluctantly abandoned the plan for wage increases through Lets pending more discussions with the tax authorities.

A business would not run into this tax problem if the worker was earning insufficient to bring them into a taxpaying bracket. Also the *ex gratia* occasional payments such as Christmas bonuses which businesses can already give to staff tax-free would incur no tax liability if paid in Lets.

Maggie believes that the tax liability from Lets earnings should be paid in Lets. In any case, she argues, their value is not equal to a pound since her staff were unwilling to accept them if they had to pay 25p in tax on each Stroud!

While negotiations continue with the Inland Revenue, the café has paid its tax bill on the basis of an estimated assessment. They have also reluctantly paid VAT based on Strouds being valued at one pound.

Maggie is now starting to develop other ways of using Lets, for example, by trying to persuade more of her suppliers to accept Strouds. 'The answer is to buy in more products locally,' she says. 'We are talking to someone who could keep chickens and sell us the eggs. We would like to persuade the local bakery who supply us to join but they hesitate because they feel they could not use the Lets they would earn. We are gradually pushing back the boundaries. The potential is so fantastic and the thing could be transformed overnight.'

Launching a business on Lets

Budding entrepreneurs seeing a niche in the market usually need labour and cash to set up. If they have savings tucked away in a bank account, or generous and wealthy relatives or friends, the necessary money may be available at a low interest rate.

If there aren't such sources of cash, the would-be business owner is thrown onto the world of venture capital, investment banks and all the other sources of start-up capital. There is much free *advice* for people wanting to set up in business, but the money available comes at a price: interest rates can be 30 per cent a year or more. Furthermore, because the investing bank is taking a risk in handing over the money, they usually ask for some sort of security, and for a substantial sum the entrepreneur's house is usually the only source of security. So you put your house on the line, and if the business booms you pay back the loan (with interest) and work and live happily. If the business fails, you lose the business ... and your home.

Chris Martley who lives outside Halifax in Yorkshire is using Lets to circumvent this difficulty. His business is intended to provide four new jobs and considerable casual work in the unemployment blackspot of the Yorkshire Moors. Three of the jobs will be taken by people who are presently unemployed, the fourth by a person who seeks to leave a low-paid part-time job.

Their partnership will involve managing and selling the output of a 20 acre wood. The capital to set up will come partly from a Forestry Commission grant which requires applicants to provide 'matching funding' from their own resources — savings or bank loans. These sums are needed to pay for buying or hiring equipment — saws, axes, woodworking tools etc. — and to pay the four partners and casual labour during the early phases. The nature of woodland management (like most businesses) is that some months of work needs to be put in before the business begins earning, and yet bills still need to be paid early on.

Chris Martley and his partners believe that by using 'Favours' on Calderdale Lets they can insulate themselves from both the risk of loss and the high cost of interest payments. They intend using the Lets units to hire the tools they need (so they need to spend out less cash buying them) and to pay the casual labourers needed in the early stages to undertake the first clearing and logging. They anticipate earning Lets by selling firewood and making and selling 'greenwood' items such as benches, bird-tables and picnic tables.

The partners do not, however, intend to abandon Lets once they are established: they expect their Lets trading to continue as the business expands.

Pubs and cabinets

In Haverfordwest, at least two businesses are trading in Lets units. The General Picton is the country's only Lets pub, where customers can buy meals for 50 per cent Lets. The owner uses some of her Lets at another local business — the Wiston Project School which teaches cabinet making. The Lets earned by the school allows its owner, Harry Wears, to buy publicity services such as desk-top publishing and photocopying for the school, and osteopathy for his son who has a bad back.

Also in Haverfordwest the local Co-operative Retail Society is a corporate member. The CRS are only dipping their toe in the water so far and their first spending on Lets has been to buy individually made prizes that they give to winners in the school competitions they promote. They are earning Lets by offering services to the Haverfordwest administrators — though they are not (yet) selling food in their stores for Lets. This, though, may come.

Commercial bartering

The success of commercial bartering companies in North America has caused the first such businesses to set up in the UK. Unlike Lets which is a community-based resource with no interest payable and no profit being made by the system (though the administrators may be paid), commercial bartering is in the big business league.

Buzz Remde of The Bartering Company says his firm has achieved a £1.8m turnover in two years of operation. 'We have 600 trading companies and they put their goods and services into the pool and can draw out goods and services of equal value, and we charge them a fee. They barter for balance sheet reasons, for bad debt recovery, and to help their cashflow.

'So a large company might make available £2m of computers and say they want airline tickets and car rental in exchange.'

The Barter Company employs brokers who set up the deals by finding the businesses with goods to trade.

Unlike Lets, The Barter Company runs as a private profit-making company, the transactions and list of members are kept confidential, those subscribing have no control over how the company runs, and they only have the opportunity to trade with other businesses, not the public.

The average transaction at The Bartering Company is £1800. To join, businesses are charged £300 a year subscription, and they pay a 10 per cent commission on everything they buy.

Businesses joining Lets are usually charged as little as £10 a year.

CHAPTER 10

Organisations and Lets

The true wealth in our community lies in the talents and services which we have to offer to one another — not in money.

The joy of Lets is that a single system can stand on its own. It requires no council grants, government permission, or input from the great and the good.

But this is not to say that input to Lets from organisations already operating in your town or community is unwelcome. On the contrary, persuading existing voluntary groups and charities, councils and development organisations to join can boost membership and make Lets more effective. Just as importantly, Lets can help these organisations with their own work.

Even in these early days of Lets, voluntary organisations and local authorities are beginning to appreciate how Local Exchange Trading Systems can be a powerful instrument for helping the economy and local communities.

In March 1994 a council in West Yorkshire became the first local authority to join Lets. A day centre in Hereford joined to buy facilities for its clients, a community development group in central London was due to launch a system based on its community centre, and the Rural Development Commission was promoting Lets in the Cotswolds to reduce unemployment in the countryside.

Local councils and Lets

The staff in Calderdale Council's Community Development Unit admit that it would be far easier for them if the authority had just given Lets a grant rather than actually join.

But Nigel Leach of Calderdale Lets was adamant that he didn't just want the council's money. He wanted them to join so they would realise and experience the benefits of Lets — and he wanted access to council services which could be paid for in Favours. Such a request led to shock waves through the council's finance department as they considered how they would record such transactions on their computers.

Despite these concerns, councillors decided they would join the system, and provide £500 worth of services which would be repaid in Lets. The council will account for the £500 worth of services by recording it as a grant.

The arrangement pleases everyone concerned — and Nigel Leach and several councillors hope it will be the thin end of a welcome wedge.

The council will keep the Favours it earns within its Community Development Department which initially will provide services to the Lets administration (not directly to the members). These services will be paid for by the system from the Favours it earns from members. The council will then use those Favours to hire Lets members to do work for other voluntary organisations and local charities — thereby increasing their grants to them.

The officers are adamant that they won't be using the Favours to buy facilities directly for the council's own use: 'If the system expands to include businesses, we would look very carefully before buying services for the council,' says council officer Rob Clegg. 'With Lets we run up against tendering issues, problems of insurance, and labour relations. We would have to be very careful.'

Rob Clegg explains that the £500 grant will be shown on the council accounts as expenditure, but that the Lets Favours are unlikely to be shown as income — although there are clearly discussions yet to be had with the treasurer's department. Other facilities and services which the council could trade on Lets raise even more problems, says Rob Clegg. Hiring school buildings, members providing computer consultancy work for council departments, a member cutting the grass on an estate: all are predicted by the officers to cause bureaucratic nightmares as the council tries to keep track of Lets spending and income across different departments. 'And if you think it will lead to people paying their council tax in Lets, then you're living on another planet,' says Rob Clegg.

But Nigel Leach takes a more optimistic view, and he points out that the councillors themselves are eyeing government restrictions on spending and are asking what the council itself can buy to reduce its reliance on bank loans and council tax.

Manchester Lets has also gained the sympathetic support of its city council. The council itself has not joined, but has supported the giving of a grant/loan through the Telematics Partnership. The Partnership has given Manchester Lets £10,000 to pay for general development costs and to find ways of allowing trading on Manchester Host, a computer network. The system intends to pay back the £10,000 in Bobbins over ten years and it is investigating setting up a development account in Lets which would be financed by businesses becoming members.

Council officers in other areas, including Telford, Oxfordshire, and Leicester, have been looking at the potential for Lets to promote jobs in depressed areas. Leicester City Council has hired the consultancy group Lets Solutions to set up systems around the city.

Often the council's Economic Development Officer has been the first to spot the opportunities, and many are proposing to their councils ways that Lets should be assisted, so that Lets jobs can be created in years to come.

Lets and TECS

Haverfordwest Lets has targeted both the local council and the Training and Enterprise Council as organisations which could benefit from involvement. Harry Wears (who co-ordinates the Haverfordwest system) wants to take over a disused school and provide construction work and training for unemployed Lets members. The aim is to refurbish the building so that it could be opened as a day nursery. Such a project requires vision and determination and at the time of writing Harry was still in discussions with the various bodies.

'Seventy per cent of our Lets members are unemployed,' says Harry Wears. 'They can't do any work on this building because to do so would put them in contravention of the social security regulations. But if the TEC funded a training scheme, people could learn construction skills, gain a National Vocational Guidance Qualification, and the building would get done up. The Lets members would do this because we could then use the building as a day nursery and a sort of Lets headquarters where we could organise projects such as a taxi service and vehicle hire on Lets.

'Nursery places cost £50 a week in Haverfordwest and we believe we could provide 20 to 30 places at £10 per week plus 40 Lets units,' he says. 'The situation with training at present is crazy: people are trained in the morning to build a brick wall. In the afternoon they kick it down, and the next day another one is built!'

Voluntary organisations

Campaigning groups, residents' associations, research networks and other organisations which rely on voluntary labour can increase the involvement of supporters using Lets.

A Lets network can comprise just the members or supporters of an organisation. Apart from the system allowing the organisation to buy particular services from supporters, it also allows members whose skills are of no direct use to the system to utilise them for the organisation's benefit. For example, a plumber's skills may be only rarely needed by the association itself, but a member hiring the plumber for a domestic job could pay the Lets units to the organisation. The buyer gets the plumbing done, the organisation receives the Lets, and the plumber has given some time to benefit an organisation s/he supports. Or a member may have equipment to hire out, or may be willing to do some work near home, while the organisation's work base is farther away.

Charities and Lets

Many charities are seriously concerned as the recession has reduced people's ability and willingness to drop coins into collecting boxes. Even in good times there is rarely enough money to meet all the demands from those in need.

The difficulty with voluntary work is matching people's time and commitment with the work the charity needs to do.

When a charity joins Lets it can sidestep some of these difficulties. It can increase the number of donors when people who do not have sterling to donate feel able either to do work directly for the charity, or to donate Lets units that they have earned from working for other people in the system. They can also attract more 'volunteers' by offering payments in Lets as recognition of work done.

Conversely, the people being helped by the charity are able to contribute too as the skills they can't sell through the job centre are often needed by Lets members. By trading through Lets, people who are spurned by the cash economy can have skills recognised, so they don't always need to be the passive recipients of charity. For example, people with disabilities using a centre in Hereford are offering house sitting for deliveries, curtain and cushion making, knitting, sewing and embroidery, and even cleaning burnt saucepans!

In return the centre hopes to buy tuition, and to pay people for taking the clients on outings.

But charities need to be a little cautious. While membership of Lets can draw more people into voluntary work and charity giving, a charity's work may not be helped if work already being done voluntarily and with good heart becomes a commercial (Lets) transaction.

Secondly, in the UK charities are prohibited by law from going into debt, and there is no case law as yet to tell us whether a high Lets commitment for a charity is something the Charity Commissioners would look on with disfavour.

Organisations in commitment

Lets and local organisations can benefit each other, but having organisations as members needs some special thought.

Lets units are created by members spending before they have

106

earned. By doing so they enter into a commitment to do some work on the system at some time in the future. The other members know who specifically has made that commitment.

When an organisation joins Lets, that commitment would come from the organisation rather than an individual. If the organisation is very large, or if there is a high turnover of members, it may be difficult to pin this commitment down.

When an organisation may seek to show itself in a good light by spending, the Lets members need to be especially cautious. Imagine the reaction if, in the run-up to an election, a council starting busily spending on the system — and the spending was mainly designed to benefit those the councillors hoped would vote for them.

One way to avoid this problem is to allow organisations to only be in credit, so the *individual* Lets members create the Lets units, and organisations such as charities, councils, and banks who join must sell before they buy. Organisations which wish to give grants in Lets would have to earn them first, either by accepting donations, or selling services. This may save the system problems in the future.

Organisations and businesses

Manchester Lets is the first in the country to have signed up a business on what is termed 'Contribution to Community'. The business joins as an ordinary member, but it also has the opportunity to add a donation which goes to a voluntary organisation of their choice.

In Manchester, Annie Kenny's, a café, has joined, and in addition to the £8 membership charge, it is also giving a donation of £40 and 40 Bobbins to Oxfam. The donation enhances the reputation of the café as a business playing a part in the community; but it also brings Oxfam into Manchester Lets. The local Oxfam office will be using the Bobbins to pay volunteers, and is likely to earn more on its account by hiring out rooms, and providing services.

Now customers can buy meals for 50% in Bobbins at the café, Oxfam may find it easier to reward volunteers, and Manchester Lets has attracted two new members.

Raising funds

Lets could potentially become an accepted route to obtaining funding for community projects.

Cash sums are available for playgrounds, community halls, vegetable growing groups, employment training, formation of co-operatives and running minibuses for the elderly. These grants come from council and government departments, the European Community, quangos, and trusts.

But often these funds have a serious drawback: the donors require those setting up the project to show there is local support by obtaining matching funding. So a request for funding for a £100,000 project will be met with the response: 'You raise £50,000 and we'll give you the other £50,000.'

- In Spring 1994 Lightmoor Village in Telford were preparing the first known example of a project application using Lets as the matching funding. Lightmoor Village does not think small, they want to build a community hall costing over a quarter of a million pounds.

  The group there built their own houses so they are confident that the labour for the hall can be found within Telford Lets and paid for with Wrekins, the local Lets unit. Hence they are asking the European Community for £187,000 and are pledging the equivalent sum in Wrekins. They cite previous applications where groups have used their own labour as matching funding, and say Lets merely formalises this procedure.

  Members anticipate that they will earn the Lets by the community centre selling food in its coffee bar, and offering conference facilities and room hire for Wrekins. Such an arrangement, in the words of John Winkworth, one of the brains behind the scheme, 'frees up the cashflow' and means the community don't need to go cap in hand to the banks to obtain a loan with a high interest rate attached.

- John Winkworth of Telford also has his eyes set on a local school. 'The school is grant maintained and is given cash for its essential needs like electricity, telephone and teachers' salaries,' he says, 'but the other things like painting and decorating and playground maintenance could be done using local money. The school could insist that tenders for this sort of work are only submitted in local money. They have all sorts of facilities which the community could use. In the holidays the school is closed, the building is isolated from the community and the staff even remove the computers from the building so as to discourage thieves. We say they could use the facilities and hire them out in Lets. They are listening!'

THANKS LUCY...
I'LL POP A LETS CHEQUE
IN THE POST

■ Telford Lets has become a member of the Telford Community Council which works to bring together community groups and charities in the Wrekin area. Together they are setting up the Waging Peace project to find employment for unemployed young people.

'The youths are going round stealing cars and the law's reaction is to lock them up or impose community service orders,' says John Winkworth. 'We say: start up a landscape or mechanics business on Lets and the unemployed youth can work for local money. They are the people at the bottom.

'At the top is the Woodside Luncheon Club which is a meeting place for professionals, many of whom have money. They are caring professional people and the Club is very interested in helping the community but most of the members have no time. Our plan is to take the youth along who have earned local money so that the professionals buy the Lets from them for cash. The youth need the cash but they also need to feel they belong and have something worthwhile to do. It's definitely going to happen!'

■ A Lets member in Penzance has plans to start up a mothers and toddlers group paid in Pecks. The aim is to base the system at her home, and charge parents in Lets units for attending. These will be the organiser's earnings for running the system.

■ In London, the community group Response was setting up Lets in Earls Court. The area has what it believes is the oldest community newspaper in Britain and Response intends to use all its local contacts to bring them into a Lets network. According to Niki Kortvellyessy, one of the management committee, they intend to pay Lets to workers in the community centre shop and to the writers who contribute to the newspaper. 'It will formalise some of the loose relationships the centre has,' says Niki. 'For instance we have to beg and plead with painters to do work for us, and paying them in Lets should make it easier to find people.' The centre also hopes to gain input from the Bosnian and Ethiopian refugee communities in the area, many of whom find it difficult to obtain conventional paid work.

Lets and trade unions

In the coming months Lets administrators will need to open discussions with trade unions to convince them that the systems can create work and are not just a ploy to undermine pay scales.

At the time of writing the UK Trades Union Congress had received no request from any of its member unions for advice on dealing with Lets. A spokesman said they would be concerned at paying employees with credits which could not be spent anywhere in the country, and they would also look carefully if the systems discouraged opportunities to bargain collectively. However the unions have made no formal decisions about their view of Lets.

CHAPTER 11

Lets and the law

And we want tax in sterling.
The chancellor will not
appreciate having his lawn
mowed.

INLAND REVENUE SPOKESWOMAN

Local Exchange Trading Systems can be set up and oper-
ated by anyone without permission from the authorities.
However the long tentacles of the law reach everywhere,
and Lets does not operate outside the law.

Lawyers trying to get to grips with the legal ramifications of
Lets rapidly realise that trying to apply current UK law to Lets is
a little like trying to apply nineteenth-century transport laws to
the aeroplane — or even the motor-car.

The chief difficulty for lawyers is the question of whether Lets
units can be legally defined as money. If they can, and it's a big
if, many current laws may affect some (but not all) of the operations of Lets. On the other hand, if Lets is not money, the courts
and authorities have considerable difficulties regulating it.

Similarly, do Lets units have any value, in the way money has
value? Or is it just a measure since members can buy whether or
not they have earned any Lets units already? If Lets units have no
value, should they count as income when considering whether a
claimant is entitled to social security payments? And, if they do
have value, is it relevant? Because in the early days of a Lets
network, it is not possible to buy many basic needs for Lets units.

Similarly, if a case involving a Lets transaction came before
a court, what redress can it order — payment of Lets in

compensation? If there was such a court order, all the defendant need do is create the Lets units to comply. And if the court cannot order the payment of Lets, and the order is for financial compensation, how will they put a value on the Lets units in terms of the national currency?

Again, if Lets is not money, what of the various regulations governing the sale of goods? Many regulations place no restrictions on transactions where no money changes hands, but impose constraints if there is financial gain.

These are just some of the questions which are likely to exercise the minds of lawyers and the courts in years to come. Lets has only been active in the UK for a few short years and as far as is known no cases involving Lets and these questions have come before any court or tribunal. Officialdom, as ever, is trying to fit Lets into conventional law, but since there is neither legislation nor case law on Lets, we will have to wait for definitive answers to some of these questions.

Consequently the answers supplied here are based on what might be the case in particular circumstances. This is not a definitive statement of the law regarding Lets, and neither the author nor the publisher can be held responsible for the accuracy of the information or the interpretation. We have no way of knowing whether courts and tribunals will interpret the law very differently.

UK law works on the cardinal principle that individuals may conduct any activity unless it is proscribed as illegal in legislation or by case law.

The legal status of Lets

There is no specific legislation restricting the running of Lets. The disappearance of local money systems was caused by the passing of the Bank Charter Act of 1844, section 10 of which reads: 'No person other than a banker who on the sixth day of May, one thousand eight hundred and forty four was lawfully issuing his own bank notes shall make or issue bank notes in any part of the United Kingdom.'

Section 11 goes on: 'It shall not be lawful for any banker to draw, accept, make or issue in England or Wales, any bill or exchange or promissory note or engagement for the payment of money payable to bearer on demand...'

Lets units exist legally because they are not banknotes: they are a measure of transactions, or a form of barter, but there are no Lets notes or coins.

Lets is an idea in the public domain: you don't need permission to set up a system, and there is no requirement to register it. There are no restrictions on the use of the terms 'Lets' and 'Local Exchange Trading Systems'.

However people attempting to set up systems which are profit-making, charging interest, or where accounts are secret, are strongly advised not to use the term Lets, not least because of the confusion which would result.

The legal status of individual systems

When people gather together for a common interest, there are a variety of legal structures available to use.

Businesses set up for profit usually opt for limited liability by shareholding; people working equally choose workers' co-operatives. Those aiming to alleviate poverty or provide education choose charitable status; while non-profitmaking businesses form companies limited by guarantee. There are also sole traders (people in business on their own) and various forms of trust.

All these structures bring different rights and responsibilities, and all are governed in some way by the law. Lets doesn't fit comfortably into any of these structures: it is not a business undertaking trading for profit or otherwise, it is not a charity, and it is not a workers' co-operative. Fortunately Lets does not need to adopt any of these structures in order to operate.

Most Lets exist without a formal legal status and remain 'unincorporated societies'. This means they have the status of a non-profitmaking private membership club and for a system operating without official grants, this status is sufficient.

RIGHT: Social Security minister Peter Lilley states that Lets credits *may* affect benefit, while the Benefits Agency says they *will*. The issue of any unfair advantages gained by Lets members would be easily solved by the authorities encouraging claimants to join their local systems.

I turn now to the particular point Mr ▆▆▆▆ has raised concerning LETS. The current IS regulations do not make any specific provision for dealing with this type of scheme, but there are a number of ways in which participating in a LETS may affect a person's IS entitlement. I should emphasise that decisions on entitlement to IS are made, in the first instance, by an independent adjudication officer (AO) in the local Benefits Agency office, and are based on the particular facts of each case. Their decisions carry a right of appeal to an independent Social Security Appeal Tribunal, with a further appeal on a point of law to the Social Security Commissioners.

The AO would first of all, need to consider whether a LETS participant was engaged in remunerative work, which for IS purposes is defined as work in which a person is engaged for, on average, 16 hours or more a week and which is done in expectation of payment. The AO may decide that participating in a LETS should be regarded as work and that the LETS credits obtained are a payment for the goods or services provided. As people who are in remunerative work are not normally eligible for IS, a person who spends more than 16 hours a week on LETS, may lose their entitlement to benefit.

PETER LILLEY

Systems are advised to have a formal members' agreement which new members should agree to before joining. This sets out the basics of how the system is to be run (see Appendix 2).

Systems applying for grants from public bodies may, however, be required to adopt a more formal status by, for example, agreeing a constitution. Manchester Lets has adopted such a constitution (see Appendix 3). An alternative model constitution suitable for a wide range of non-profitmaking societies is available from the National Council for Voluntary Organisations (see Appendix 4).

However, systems considering going down this road should remember that administrators can theoretically be challenged in the courts for not complying with the provisions of a constitution.

Data Protection Registry

The Data Protection Act regulates the use of information about individuals held on computer, and in particular, restricts how such information is distributed.

Organisations such as businesses and constituted organisations such as charities are required to register with the Data Protection Registrar and to comply with various conditions.

Most Lets networks are unincorporated societies. Where these hold information about members on computer, they are exempt from having to register provided that all members (including new members) are asked for their permission for the information about them to be held on computer. The members also have to give their permission for the information to be disclosed. It is best for this permission to be given in writing.

The Registrar recommends that unincorporated societies such as Lets identify the circumstances in which they might wish to disclose the information and ask members for the appropriate permission. For Lets these are likely to be revealing the statements of account to members, and publishing the directory to members (and to the general public for advertising purposes). This would mean members' balances could not be released to non-members, but the directory could be used to demonstrate the worth of the system to people interested in joining.

The requirement for consent to be given applies to both the

information on the computer, and any paperwork such as the directory and accounts statements generated from the computer record.

A system which revealed information about its members without asking for permission would be committing a criminal offence.

If a member objects to information about themselves being maintained on computer, their details should be processed manually; or the club should register with the Registrar in which case the information may be held on computer whether a member objects or not.

The model agreement (see Appendix) contains the relevant clauses for consent.

If a system adopts a legal status other than an unincorporated society, it is likely to have to register.

Advertising

The British Code of Advertising Practice is a voluntary code covering advertising in newspapers, magazines, etc. The code broadly requires advertisements to be 'legal, decent, honest and truthful'. Editors of Lets directories are advised to ensure advertisements from members conform to these standards.

Advertisements from businesses

The Business Advertisements (Disclosure) Order 1977 requires traders offering goods and services for sale in advertisements to declare they are operating as a business.

Entries in Lets directories should therefore make it clear whether a person offering goods and services for sale is doing so by means of their trade.

Income tax

The Inland Revenue state that any income, from whatever source, must be declared on annual tax returns. They say that Lets units constitute income and so, strictly speaking, all Lets units earned should be declared on tax returns and expressed in terms of their sterling value.

You just can't fiddle on Lets

The owner of one business said: 'It has been suggested to us that Lets has just been set up so we can fiddle our taxes. In fact, it is far, far easier for us to pay casual workers cash in hand and avoid tax, than it is to do the same on Lets. For all Lets transactions are recorded on the accounts, and those accounts are available for all members to see. Lets cannot be part of the black market, it simply isn't possible to pay over Lets without it being recorded in the books, for the transaction only exists by being recorded on the accounts.'

However, the Inland Revenue say tax is unlikely to be payable if the transactions are small-scale and of an occasional nature. This means that if the Lets earnings were part of a business, tax would be payable on the profits. Thus a plumber offering plumbing work on Lets would have to pay tax on the total Lets and sterling profits. But a plumber doing the occasional driving or gardening is unlikely to have to pay tax on these transactions.

Conversely, where a business expense is normally allowable against tax, if that expense has been incurred in Lets, the taxpayer can declare the sterling value of the purchase as an expense, and set it against their profits.

We have no experience of the tax implications of formally employing people for Lets and the ramifications for employers' and employees' income tax, and national insurance contributions. However employers only have to deduct national insurance when an employee's income is over £57 per week, and income tax when it is over £66.50 per week, and thus Lets credits under these figures would not enmesh employers or employees in extensive paperwork.

For any transaction where income tax is likely to be due on the earnings, the seller is advised to charge the tax percentage of the cost of the job in sterling to cover the income tax element.

Where a Lets unit is on a par with the pound, the member should convert the credits into sterling on the tax return. Where the Lets unit is not tied to the pound the member will need to reach agreement with the local tax office on the value.

Any tax due, according to the Inland Revenue, must be paid in sterling: it cannot be paid in the local Lets unit.

The system itself is under no obligation to declare members' Lets earnings to the Inland Revenue, nor are administrators obliged to release names of members. There are legal procedures that the Inland Revenue can follow to require a bank or other financial institution to reveal the account details of a specific customer: Lets administrators are advised to require the Inland Revenue to follow the same procedure if they require details of a specific account if the member refuses to permit its disclosure.

Since the Lets network itself is non-profitmaking, there are unlikely to be any tax implications for the system itself.

Where administrators are paid fees in Lets the same rules apply as for other types of work.

Negotiations with the Inland Revenue are at a very early stage. Members who have declared Lets income and outgoings have, in the main, merely incorporated them into their sterling income so the local tax inspector often does not even know that some part of the accounts relate to Lets.

Businesses such as Mills Café in Stroud (see Chapter 9) which has turned over 35,000 Strouds are still negotiating. No precedents have been set in the courts as to the value of the units, nor even whether tax can be paid in Lets — which would be the appropriate way of paying. (The government already accepts the precedent that taxes need not always be paid in sterling — it will sometimes accept payment of death duties in the form of historic houses and their contents.)

How much is a job really worth?

The Inland Revenue say that tax is due on all profits from business or trade, while the amount due for Lets work is based on what the job would have cost if it had been paid in sterling. Hence they demand that taxpayers convert the Lets units to pounds for declaration on the tax return.

However this recipe takes no account of jobs carried out on Lets which would simply not have been done at all if the charge had been in sterling. So, for example, saying that repairing an old vacuum cleaner earned the repairer £30 when the charge was 30 Lets is quite misleading when the machine may only have been valued at, say £10, and most owners would not dream of paying three times that sum to have it repaired.

There is thus a strong argument for saying that the job is only worth in sterling what the buyer would have been prepared to pay, rather than the normal commercial rate for doing the job. Taxpayers wishing to advance the cause of Lets may wish to put this argument to their local tax office — any resulting negotiations are likely to be very interesting!

In addition to possibly achieving a more realistic tax assessment, taking such issues into account may act to encourage the carrying out of repairs which are often environmentally better than wholesale replacement.

Charitable covenants

Where an income tax payer enters into a covenant to pay a regular sum to a registered charity, the income tax paid can be recovered by the charity in addition to the regular payments. Despite the Inland Revenue regarding Lets credits as profits on which tax is payable, they state that Lets covenanted to a charity would not allow the charity to claim back the tax because such donations have to be in 'money'. However there have been no cases of a taxpayer and charity attempting to do this, and the issue would need to come to appeal for a precedent to be set.

Value Added Tax

Where a trader is registered for VAT, this element of all transactions — including those in Lets — must be charged in sterling. It would be an offence for a trader registered for VAT not to collect the VAT portion in sterling. The trader must then declare and pay the VAT collected to Customs and Excise in the normal way.

Social security

Members who are also claimants need to be aware that current Social Security regulations are both complex and less than clear about how working for Lets should affect benefit. The

Department of Social Security (which decides the policy) and the Benefits Agency (which administers the payments) say the regulations mean that Lets credits constitute earnings. This interpretation has not fully clarified the issue because local Benefits Agency offices have not been adopting a consistent approach to dealing with claimants on Lets.

The position is only likely to become clear as a body of precedents is built up through adjudication and as claimants appeal to the social security tribunals.

In the meantime, claimants need to be aware that the situation regarding benefits is unclear although existing regulations do allow small amounts of earnings to be received without benefits being affected.

Income support

Income Support is payable to claimants who are not working more than 16 hours a week, in most cases are available for and actively seeking work, and whose income and capital are below certain amounts. Most claimants on IS are able to earn up to £5 per week (known as the disregard limit) without their benefit being affected; any earnings over this are deducted pound for pound. Single parents, pensioners and sick and disabled people (among others) are allowed to earn up to £15 per week, and there are some special regulations covering income from childminding, providing board and lodgings, etc.

Therefore a Lets member on IS should not undertake Lets work which takes 16 hours or more a week. They should continue to actively seek work if that is already a condition they have to meet, and preferably ask anyone for whom they are performing a Lets service to sign a 'release document' saying they can leave immediately if any work becomes available. Thirdly, any Lets credits below an equivalent of £5 per week are unlikely to affect benefit, although the Benefits Agency could decide that payments received 'are unreasonable for the service' and deduct benefit as though they were greater.

The authorities state that Lets credits constitute earnings according to the regulations, and therefore any work on Lets should be declared regardless of the level of earnings. Benefit will be reduced for any Lets credits received over the disregard limits.

There are slightly different regulations defining earnings for claimants who are employed or self-employed.

For those employed, earnings are 'any renumeration or profit derived from that employment', while for the self-employed it is the net profits which are taken into account. Net profits are the earnings less 'any expenses wholly and exclusively defrayed ... for the purposes of that employment'.

The authorities make their ruling that Lets units constitute income despite regulations which say that 'payments or income in kind' are not regarded as earnings. Although this is not defined in the actual regulations, a Benefits Agency handbook lists 'food, meals, cigarettes' and, interestingly, 'luncheon vouchers' as 'types of income which are ignored completely' when deciding whether IS payments should be reduced.

Where the Lets unit is not equivalent to the pound, the adjudication officer could ascribe a value to the service performed, if not to the actual Lets units.

Particular expenses

In Telford the local Lets administrator was told the Lets credits she received for administering the system would not affect her benefit. In this case the Claimant Adviser interpreted the Lets payments as 'expenses' paid by a charity or voluntary organisation which are normally ignored when assessing benefit: 'any payment in respect of any expenses incurred by a claimant who is engaged by a charitable or voluntary body or a volunteer if he otherwise derives no renumeration or profit from the employment'.

A community worker was told by Benefits Agency officials in the north east that provided Lets members signed a declaration stating they were receiving no financial benefit their IS payments would not be affected provided they were still actively seeking work and undertaking Lets services for under 16 hours a week. The officials said the declaration would protect a claimant against anonymous accusations that they were illegally working.

In the East Midlands, administrators were told that if a claimant performed Lets services which were not part of their normal occupation, the credits would be ignored. Thus Lets units received by a plumber for doing babysitting would not affect benefit, but credits for plumbing work would.

However the Benefits Agency nationally say such decisions are wrong and that Lets income will result in deductions of benefit over the disregard limits.

Unemployment benefit

Similar rules apply to the payment of unemployment benefit. Claimants must declare any work they do and any earnings over £2 per day will cause the unemployment benefit for that day to be stopped. This includes Lets work and Lets credits.

Invalidity benefit

Invalidity Benefit is paid to claimants who are unable to work because of their poor health. They do not have to be available for, nor actively seeking, work. If the Benefits Agency concludes the claimant is, in fact, able to work, they can stop the payment of invalidity benefit.

However the Agency may (but does not have to) ignore payments of up to £42 per week if the work is carried out under medical supervision as part of hospital treatment, or where the claimant has 'good cause' to do the work. Social Security Commissioners have decided that where work is recommended by a doctor or social worker for therapeutic reasons, then it is done for 'good cause', although in general if it is just done for more income, it is not.

If the Agency does decide to ignore this work, the invalidity benefit or severe disablement allowance is paid as though the person was doing no work at all.

People on invalidity benefit considering offering services on Lets are advised to first consult their doctor or social worker and obtain a letter stating the Lets work would be therapeutic for them.

Why the DSS should support Lets

Lets administrators considering holding meetings with their local Benefits Agency officers should stress its considerable potential for creating jobs by assisting new and existing local businesses and thereby in the long run reducing the need for social security payments.

Lets can benefit the economy by directly allowing new businesses to open, by helping people without sterling to start in trade, and by keeping an otherwise ailing business in existence as it gains access to a new source of customers.

As such, Lets addresses a fundamental drawback of the existing benefits system: that in a world of insufficient full-time jobs, the DSS rules prevent claimants testing the market and building up their own small businesses before coming off benefit. Either a claimant is unemployed, or they are employed, and the regulations take little account of the fact that many claimants would be able to find their way into work if they could do it by building up gradually. Lets allows them to do so without earning sterling.

Lets can also help claimants into jobs by allowing them to use their credits to commission professionally produced CVs and gain jobs counselling, training in interview skills, and to learn new marketable skills. Being involved in Lets also allows a claimant to keep in touch with the world of work, and to maintain a positive attitude which is essential if they are to keep seeking jobs.

Despite their ruling, it can be argued that the DSS should not regard Lets credits as income since the units have no value in themselves, no money changes hands, and having Lets units in an account doesn't allow a member any advantage over another who is in minus: both are able to spend. There's the further issue that in the early life of Lets groups, members would generally find it difficult to buy many of the bare necessities of life for Lets — and it is these needs which social security payments are intended to cover. These limits on the use of Lets in the early life of systems are implicitly accepted by the Inland Revenue which refuses to accept Lets credits for tax payments.

The Australian Minister for Social Security, Peter Baldwin, has seen the benefits that Lets can bring. In a statement, he said: 'Lets type schemes are a useful community initiative which should not be artificially discouraged by social security arrangements. They represent a form of activity that assists our clients in keeping in contact with labour market skills and habits and with the labour market itself.'

To reinforce this view he ruled that Lets credits would not affect claimants' access to social security payments as long as they continued to actively seek work.

Environmental health

The regulations requiring various standards to be maintained when preparing cooked food for sale apply only to sales to the general public.

When sales of cooked food are only to members of a private society such as Lets, suppliers are not required either to have their premises inspected by environmental health officers, or to adopt particular standards.

Members offering cooked food for sale on Lets are nevertheless recommended to be aware of the regulations so proper standards of hygiene are observed.

IT'S LEGAL ... BUT

Following the law when deciding what services are acceptable to offer on Lets could lead members in directions they might not intend to go.

Exchanging a few bottles of home-made wine on the Lets network is unlikely to be frowned upon by society, but this would actually be illegal on two counts: because the wine would be sold without the payment of excise duty, and because it would be done without a licence.

Conversely, however, a service which would be legal on Lets, but socially less acceptable, would be prostitution. Prostitutes can only be prosecuted for soliciting (seeking customers for sex in a public place), not the actual selling of sex. Lets administrators would be unlikely to be guilty of the separate offence of living off immoral earnings because the system is non-profitmaking (even though the administrators may be paid), and because attempts to prosecute even pornographic magazines for advertising sexual services have failed in the past.

However, while prostitutes might feel that Lets could be just the place to offer sex services with a degree of safety — because they would know something of their clients — most members would say this is unlikely to enhance the reputation of the Lets network!

125

Trade and professional qualifications

Many occupations now require practitioners to have appropriate qualifications before they are allowed to carry on employment in these jobs.

Occupations where practitioners are governed by law include architects, dentists, opticians, doctors and other medical occupations, patent agents, pharmacists, solicitors and vets. Other occupations, such as gas fitters, electricians, and actors, are regulated by the relevant professional or trade bodies.

The effect of these regulations is that it is legal for people to do these jobs for themselves, and they can carry some of them out as favours for other people; but they have to comply with the rules when offering to do the work for money or for the general public.

There is no case law setting precedents to say whether working for Lets would require members to be suitably qualified, or whether they could claim they were merely undertaking social favours.

However members considering practising any occupation for which they are not suitably qualified are advised to consult the relevant regulations and comply with the spirit of them.

As systems mature, the issue of whether the various regulations extend to include Lets transactions will be decided as cases come before the courts.

Liability for poor quality work

When someone agrees to do a job they are bound by law to use reasonable skill and care, and if they don't, they can be sued for breach of contract for any loss. If, in addition, property is damaged or a person is injured, they can be sued for negligence.

This applies to work undertaken for money, but if the job had been carried out as a favour, the plaintiff would not normally be able to claim there had been any loss unless some property had been damaged by the work. No cases involving poor quality work done on Lets have come before the courts but in such cases the question to be decided would be whether the plaintiff's payment of the Lets credits constituted a resultant loss.

Actions for poor work are brought in the county court, and to succeed the court would have to be satisfied that the plaintiff had suffered loss and that this loss could be compensated with money. It is debatable whether a court could order a defendant to pay back Lets units, although with small claims of under £1000 in value the county courts try to reach an arbitrated settlement — and this could involve advising that Lets units are refunded.

Lets members who are unable to gain satisfaction from a person who performed a job badly would be better advised to seek help from the group's stewards or advisers rather than sueing in the county court.

Selling the produce of allotments

The provision of allotments in the UK by local councils is governed by the 1922 Allotments Act. The aim of the act was to allow 'the labouring poor' to grow fruit and vegetables for their own consumption.

The relevant section of the Act states that an allotment is a piece of land 'which is wholly or mainly cultivated by the occupier for the production of vegetable or fruit crops for consumption by himself or his family'. This clause is generally built into tenancy agreements by including a requirement that the allotment shall not be used for the purpose of any trade or business.

Thus it is within the Act for allotment occupiers to dispose of surpluses provided the majority of the crop is for their personal consumption and the sale or exchange is not part of a business. Lets members should check their tenancy agreements because they may specify that produce may not be sold at all.

Neither the Allotments Act nor the typical tenancy agreement governs whether the surplus is disposed of for pounds, for barter or for Lets.

Allotment holders wishing to sell vegetables or fruit on Lets should therefore ensure they are only disposing of surpluses and that they are not engaged in a business.

Vehicle insurance

Most private motor vehicle insurance policies specify that, while a driver may receive money to cover the expenses of giving a lift, the receipt of any profit could make the policy invalid and leave the driver without the legally required cover.

The Association of British Insurers says that even the payment of a couple of pounds for a driver's time could constitute profit, but warn that since Lets is so new, they cannot predict how insurance companies would view the provision of occasional lifts for Lets. They advise members proposing to offer driving for Lets to tell their insurance company so they can make a decision about how the policy might be affected.

Residential tenancies

The occupier of a residential property paying rent in Lets credits is likely to have security of tenure where the owner does not live on the premises. Security is gained when there is a contract (even verbally) and money, work or payments in kind are given for the occupancy. It is likely, therefore, that Lets units would bring the same right of security. (There is no security when the owner lives on the premises.)

Alcoholic drinks

It is illegal to sell or barter home-made alcoholic drinks without paying duty or without a licence, or to sell manufactured alcoholic drinks without a licence. According to Customs and Excise, it would be similarly illegal to sell home-made wine or beer on Lets.

Inheritance

Strict laws govern what happens to a person's estate when they die. Executors have to follow a precise procedure for paying any debts outstanding before the estate can be divided among the beneficiaries.

If a Lets member has stated in their will that their Lets credits should be given to a particular person, there is no reason why this transfer should not go ahead: the Lets administrators can be satisfied that they are making the transfer on the directions of the account holder. If the deceased has made no clear instruction it may be that a general proviso at the end of the will stating that the residue of the estate should be given in a particular way would cover the Lets transfer.

However, where there is no direction in the will, there is no easy guide to what happens to credits. There are, at this stage, no legal precedents to draw on.

Similarly if a person dies with a minus balance it is unlikely that the administrators could claim against the estate — for how would the commitment be met? It is in the nature of Lets that a commitment cannot be 'discharged' by a payment in sterling from the estate.

Since Lets is primarily a community resource, the most comfortable approach, if there are no directions in the will, would be for the person's account to be simply closed. If a beneficiary of the will is already a Lets member, it might be courteous to offer any credits to them, or request their support for giving them to a charity or similar organisation.

CHAPTER 12

Still a rough ride in places

A bargain is an agreement
where both parties are happy
that they have got the best deal.

SUJOY SRIMAL,
CALCUTTA EQUITABLE
MARKETING ASSOCIATION

L ets is the sort of idea that prompts people to ask why no
one had invented it before. Easy to set up without any
outside help, it combines economic activity with social
benefit, and it appeals across class and cultural divides.

Yet even Lets groups have their problems and controversies.
Lets has only been around for a few short years, and we are still
learning about how it works. We will only know the answers to
some of the questions when Lets reaches some sort of maturity
with hundreds of thousands of people trading.

We learn by using our imagination and by experimenting.
Here Lets has an advantage over the world of mainstream
banking. For since Lets networks are closed systems which are
easily understood by the participants, members have the opportunity to experiment. If we want to see what happens by
introducing a certain innovation, we just try it out on our own
system. The lessons we learn will be as valuable as those learnt
by economists using sophisticated computer modelling to simu-
late the mainstream economy of national currencies. For — as
long as your fellow members agree — the structure of Lets can be

adapted to provide solutions best suited to your area when innovations are suggested or problems appear.

The question of equivalence

Perhaps the most controversial issue, at least among some Lets activists, is the question of whether the Lets unit should be equivalent in value to the national currency — one Lets unit being equal in value to one pound, dollar or whatever.

In an earlier chapter we listed the advantages and disadvantages to your fledgling system of the different approaches to valuation. There may, however, be considerable ramifications for Lets as a whole if systems decide to go down the equivalence road rather than another.

Michael Linton, who designed the LETSystem in 1983, takes the most determined view. According to Michael, if a group of people don't make their unit equivalent to the national currency unit, then they have not set up a LETSystem, they have set up what he terms a 'personal money' network. 'This isn't a matter of opinion,' he says. 'If the Lets unit is not equivalent, it is not a LETSystem.'

However according to a recent survey by LetsLink, while nearly two thirds of groups have linked their Lets unit to the pound, over a third of networks in the UK have deliberately set a different value for their unit in order to divorce it entirely from the mainstream economy. Many members believe it is the very ethos of Lets that it is a community resource available for local people to use in their areas as they think best.

Michael Linton's company Landsman argues that it is only by plugging Lets into the world of national currencies that businesses will be able to join. Since most trading is carried on through businesses and Lets is such an effective tool for economic and environmental regeneration, Landsman argues that businesses have to join for Lets to realise its full potential.

It is true that if businesses join Lets they are encouraged to buy in more of their stock from local suppliers, and to spend more of their profits in the local economy. Indeed a business trading in Lets may be able to avoid some (but not all) of the criticisms levelled at our increasingly uncaring and distant business sector.

The multiLETS registry

But the issue of equivalence has also to be seen in the light of another pressure within Lets. The great advantage of Lets units is that they can typically only be spent locally. But while this benefits the local community economy, the restriction can also be a disadvantage. As systems are growing in number there are more in a locality, and participants are beginning to find they have two or even more systems within reach.

They also want to spend Lets in more distant systems. Perhaps they want to go on holiday to another part of the country and a Lets member at their destination has a holiday cottage available. Or they are in a city, and a system in the nearby countryside has members who sell fresh vegetables for Lets. Or, like many people, they live in one place and work several miles away and want to belong to systems in both areas.

There is therefore pressure to trade between systems. In Wiltshire two systems have set up a reciprocal trading agreement where they accept each other's cheques.

Landsman is promoting what it terms 'multiLETS' where different systems set up a central regional register which does the accounts for many systems in local areas. Such an arrangement would allow new groups to form without the complication of having to maintain the accounts: they only have to produce their own directory. Within this overall structure it is easier for members to trade with each other if the different Lets units have a common value — that is equivalence to the pound. Manchester and Telford are both developing multiLETS for their areas.

Dangers of trading across systems

If we could go back several thousand years we might just find that this is a familiar story. Money develops for local trading, becomes useful for trading over distance, and rapidly becomes a commodity being traded for its own value, with less available for trading in needed resources.

Could this happen to Lets? It could indeed, according to Paul Ekins of Birkbeck College and The New Economics Foundation. He predicts that if different Lets currencies are interchangeable, 'substantial Lets holdings could accrue to account holders from outside the community. Exchange rates between Lets schemes

Suzanne Dunstan cleans windows on Exeter Lets. *Photo: Paul Edwards*

would fluctuate according to perceived differences in variety and quality of the goods and services on offer in each.'

The result, he says, would be speculation in Lets currencies on the basis of these fluctuations in exchange rates. 'In short, convertibility would eventually lead to Lets schemes re-enacting on a local level all the contortions of the international financial markets.'

However it can be argued that it would be difficult to 'sell' Lets units at a premium because, unlike conventional money, they are not scarce, since they can be created at will.

Certainly ring-fencing Lets units will keep the operations simple, and ensure that Lets keeps delivering its main benefit of helping the local economy and recreating the sense of community we have lost. But it may restrict its potential.

Larger businesses will become interested in joining when they perceive that Lets groups provide an extensive customer base whose purchasing power is being diverted elsewhere. When that happens a proportion of their income which at present flies outside the area will remain to be spent locally if the Lets units cannot be used elsewhere.

But such businesses may be motivated more by public relations concerns than a desire to benefit the local economy. A supermarket could reduce criticism it faces over a new development by 'demonstrating' its community commitment by selling a handful of lines for a small percentage of Lets on quiet days when few people actually go shopping. If this blunts the increasing criticism of such stores, Lets will not have performed a useful service.

Thus whether or not your Lets unit is tied to the national currency may have far-reaching consequences.

Is Lets just a product of the recession?

Will Lets cease to be attractive to people in a more buoyant economy because they will be able to enjoy spending pounds again? This is the view of several media commentators: indeed it is the first conclusion many journalists come to when writing about Lets. However it ignores the great social benefits which members would be loth to lose.

This is not to say that people join to increase their social network, more that Lets allows them to combine business with pleasure, and the economic transactions become more valued because there is often a social element. This aspect alone may be enough to ensure Lets survives any recovery in the mainstream economy.

Lets is also highly likely to outlast recession because even when modern economies recover, they still leave increasing numbers of people without adequate work, and huge numbers without fulfilling work. Lets, of course, allows people to diversify easily and have more control over their work, and to claim that the people who benefit from Lets are only those suffering from the recession is a fallacy: many value the networks because they plainly see the serious drawbacks of relying exclusively on national currencies.

Also many people working for social and environmental change are less than convinced that the economy will ever really recover: they believe we are locked into boom and bust cycles where there are fewer people in employment after each bust period. Coupled with the underlying environmental causes of recession (the economic and social effects of global warming, soil degradation, water pollution, and over-consumption of finite resources) there is a real possibility that we are heading towards the crash of all crashes. In such circumstances it is wise for people to ensure that they have some trading arrangements in place which can function even after governments entirely lose control of the mainstream economy. Some might say this is a domesday scenario, but there is increasing concern that damage to the environment and the relationship between the First and Third World countries will soon force us into a 'post industrial age' in which an alternative trading structure will be essential. And apart from Lets, nearly all economic activity relies on national currencies.

Lets and the better off

Most Lets trading is in the form of services: time spent decorating, repairing washing machines, servicing the car, childminding, housesitting etc. But just as useful are the loans of equipment and buildings available on Lets networks. Caravans for rent, halls for hire, holiday cottages, even offices and rooms in shared houses are available in some places.

Some of these 'surplus' possessions can only be acquired in the first place by a person who is relatively well off. Thus the owner of a hall in one large city is potentially able to earn large amounts of Lets units by renting out their building. The situation raised a few hackles when some members felt the sum being charged was rather high. Another view is that the owner of the building is being community minded by allowing a valuable resource to be taken out of the sterling economy for some part of the week.

It is argued by some that Lets is doing nothing to redress extremes of wealth, since the more affluent members can achieve even more wealth by renting out property or equipment for Lets.

But, and it's a big but, it has to be remembered that when someone less wealthy is being asked to pay Lets to someone more wealthy, the transaction is unlike sterling in that Lets is not a scarce resource. The person with less money can create the units to pay the bill simply by writing the cheque. Yes, they do enter into a commitment to do some work on Lets in the future, but they aren't dependant on already being in possession of scarce sterling and they don't have to pay any interest as a result.

Conversely a person who receives high numbers of Lets units is not necessarily becoming 'richer'. The Lets units are only of use if they can be spent: they can't be invested, or lent for interest. Indeed someone with a large number of units they can't spend is actually quite poor.

There are also signs that there are wealthy people who feel grave disquiet about the crazy economics which governs our world, and they want to be part of the building of a new economy.

Lets and revaluing work

Lets is widely praised for revaluing work. As people join systems they are increasingly putting new values on jobs. Work which is unattractive because it is dangerous or dirty can earn more than if done in pounds because members are more prepared to accept that it should be better rewarded.

This revaluing applies especially to work done by women. In

national currencies, work done by women is generally paid at a lower rate than traditional men's jobs. Indeed much work done by women is not paid at all. Many women in Lets particularly value the opportunity to have their work paid at a more realistic rate, and because fellow members create the Lets credits, they are often better able to pay this rate than if they were reliant on scarce pounds.

As Lets becomes bigger there is a danger that the unskilled jobs which attract low pay in the mainstream economy will attract similar rates in Lets groups. However the danger may not be as great, because the signs are that many members will pay more to someone for work which is conventionally low paid because they know something about the person, and they are not making hard decisions how to allocate the scarce resource of a national currency.

Many people also possess a certain egalitarian streak, and although they may not want everyone to be paid the same, they often don't approve of the huge differences between the very high earners and the poor. National currencies take no account of these feelings, while Lets can allow them to emerge.

The expenses of a Lets job

There is one area of work which Lets fails to address, and this is the spending which a Lets member incurs in order to do some Lets work.

Parents who charge four Lets units for an hour's gardening are no better off if they have to pay four Lets an hour to a babysitter while the gardening is done. Similarly a person in a wheelchair who has to pay Lets for a lift to someone's house where they are to do some typing may also barely benefit.

So far, systems have not seriously addressed this problem which can put off many people for whom Lets could be highly beneficial.

There are four routes to solving the problem — but none is ideal.

1 The person needing the extra Lets for doing a job can charge them to the buyer. This arrangement is simple and does not

lead the system into the problems found in the other alternatives. Its disadvantage is clearly that people charging, say, double for a job because they have to pay a babysitter could price themselves out of the market. They may not entirely price themselves out, because some members may choose to employ someone because they have disabilities and they know the work would be welcome. But other members may go to someone cheaper.

2 The system sets up a Lets fund to which all members contribute a percentage of their turnover, and this fund pays for expenses incurred by those having 'special needs' such as babysitters or lifts. Such an arrangement changes Lets from a resource where members pay just the cost of servicing their account, to a bureaucracy which is levying a 'tax' to fund social security expenditure. If you go down this road, be careful: some potential members may be put off even if your existing members believe it is right for them to help those less advantaged than themselves. The advantage of this arrangement is that the extra needs of some members are collectively provided for by the whole network.

3 Establish an account which funds such needs, but which goes into minus and is topped up by donation. In effect you are just running a charity on the system. The administrators will need to appeal regularly for Lets credits to prevent this account from going too far into minus.

4 This is the anarchic approach: establish an account which pays out for such special needs, but which shows on the accounts as an ever increasing minus.

It could be argued that this debit will be not dissimilar to a minus shown if a member leaves the system with a high minus which is not brought back to zero. That is, no one loses, the trading continues, and the presence of a high minus figure on the accounts is accepted by the members.

However, although existing members may fully understand the wisdom of such an account and agree with it, a high minus could be seen by others in the future as indicating that the system is not properly organised. Once again such a minus account is likely to matter if members think it matters. If they don't, then this may be a valid way of dealing with this problem.

Only experience will show the effect of running such an account, and the consequences may vary from place to place.

Lets and the severely disabled

A common fear among prospective members is that they aren't able to do any work which other members are likely to want. For most people this fear is unfounded, and a look at the Inspiration List (see Appendix 1) will show how people are exercising great ingenuity in offering different trades.

However there will be some people who aren't able to meet commitments. These are likely to include people with severe disabilities, the chronically sick, and many elderly people who are already being supported by society either through charity or state benefits, but who are also excluded from many of society's activities.

A system which doesn't take these people's needs into account cannot fairly claim to be a community resource. Yet within the basic design of Lets there are no structures for people who are really unable to meet a commitment and who genuinely cannot be economically active.

Members need to make a decision on this: and the options are really the same as the ones outlined above. Either your system grows into a 'government' levying a 'tax' to underwrite the purchasing done by people with disabilities, or the system runs a charity account which members are invited to donate to, or an account is run which goes severely (and for ever) into minus.

Again little is known about the effects of running such accounts.

Problems of the workload

Sooner or later a member suggests that instead of writing cheques and sending them in for some poor soul to keep totting up, why not just issue tokens? Or to put it another way, wouldn't it be easier for the members to produce their own money?

A dangerous thought! Local money used to be popular in Britain and some was still in circulation as late as the 1920s. Such money was centrally issued by a local government or a private company, and was made illegal because of the way those forming the money could dictate its value and the effect on the national currency.

A further difficulty arises if Lets ceases to be accounts-based. The amount of wealth we accrue in the world of sterling is regulated by the government limiting how many pounds are in circulation. The amount of wealth we accrue (or how greedy we are) in the world of Lets is regulated by our local community knowing how much we are in commitment. If we individually just created money in the form of a token or note when we bought on Lets, there would be no regulation possible because no one would know how much buying and selling individuals were doing. (It doesn't matter that on some systems many members have no interest in other people's spending patterns; the important point is that they have the opportunity to know if they want to.)

A second possibility is to ask whether it is necessary for the transactions to be recorded at all. Why don't the members just undertake the transactions without deciding on any prices at all, and therefore without issuing cheques or having the units recorded by the administrators? In other words why don't people just list favours they will do for each other?

In the long term some systems may well run on this basis. But in the short term it is likely that many people would be reluctant to join a system running this way. For most of us, our attachment to the money economy is too strong: the recording of transactions to ensure 'fairness' is needed to satisfy people that they can have confidence in the system.

Can a system die?

At a time when systems are springing up across Britain at the rate of more than one a week, this may seem an unwelcome question. But just as we should all make a will, we should also give some thought to a system dying.

Such an event may occur because the members lose enthusiasm and the trading stagnates, or because the administrators do a poor job, the directory doesn't appear, and the accounts are barely kept up.

The rare cases where this seems to have happened are where a system was announced, there was a short flurry of activity, and then the core members lost enthusiasm.

The result (since little trading is likely to have been done) is that no one really loses out because no one is likely to have been left with a high number of Lets units which they then can't spend.

Another difficulty might be when a member builds up a very large minus by spending Lets units fairly equally among most or all of the other members. This is possible, though unlikely, but the result of the member departing might be the unusual one of the majority of remaining members having high numbers of Lets units which discourages them from taking on any more work. The result might be to stagnate the system: but again, it's possible that members will still continue trading because they are committed to Lets in a way they are not committed to a national currency.

Much ado about nothing

According to Harry Wears who runs Haverfordwest Lets, 'All this stuff about the accounts having to add up to zero is really a nonsense. We have decided to have a currency with no interest, no fixed time to pay back, and no buying and selling of currency, so why do we need to say it has to add up to zero? Lets is an enabling device, it's a measure, and to say the transactions have to add to zero means we are looking at it as though it is normal banking. We should be highlighting the difference between Lets and sterling.'

Harry's attitude to zero led him to try and persuade his Lets group to 'give' 1000 units to each of their members. He only partially succeeded, and the group gave 100 Lets units (equivalent to £100) to members as a way of persuading them there is no debt in Lets.

If a system does not introduce a 'social services' account which goes into minus, and does not run its system account into minus, there is no reason why all the trading should not add up to zero in the early days of operation. That is, all the plus figures in the accounts will cancel out the minus figures so the total of all accounts is zero. But careful checking will show that over time, despite the best intentions, discrepancies will creep in. Simple mistakes in adding up, people leaving in minus or plus, fluctuations in the system account and other influences are likely to mean that, in reality, the trading won't actually add to zero.

Most systems may not even know this is happening since there is no real reason to count up all the balances: there is no annual audit required, no accounts have to be filed, and the system does not need to ensure it is not trading while insolvent.

The problem is that while, at first sight, it may not matter that the accounts do not add up to zero, deliberately moving away from the goal could open up the floodgates. For if adding to zero doesn't matter, the system might as well run a generous social services account for single parents and people with disabilities. It might as well give lump sums of Lets to the people who set up the system. It could help charities by giving them sizeable amounts of Lets units as donations. By forever creating Lets credits such a system would move away from the key principle that members create Lets by committing themselves to do some work on the system to that value in the future.

At the present stage of development of Lets we don't know whether releasing the floodwaters will lead to a loss of confidence in the Lets units as the importance of the commitment to bring accounts back to zero is undermined. The only way we will find out is to try the different options. But if your system is deliberately going to depart from the zero option, do so with your eyes wide open.

A sell-by date

Penzance Lets has discussed putting a 'sell-by date' on Lets credits. Their logic is that they want to persuade people to spend, for it is the spending which drives the system and contributes to its success. They specifically don't want people hoarding or saving their Lets units, and so they have been considering wiping out credits held beyond six months or a year.

What would be the likely consequences of this? Firstly there would be considerably more work for the administrators of the Lets accounts as they ensured only credits held beyond the set period were wiped. Secondly there would be some difficulty in ensuring the system worked reliably when it wiped credits clean. Thirdly there would be some opposition from members when they realised that credits were going to be wiped from their account, but not minus balances! Next there would be the problem of where those Lets units went to: would they go into a black hole and, if so, what would be the effect of this?

Indeed when members think their credits are going to be wiped clean, the effect might be the opposite of what is intended, in that they refuse to take on any more work until they've spent what they've already earned.

One way of making members feel less unhappy about 'losing their wealth' (as it would be seen) could be to transfer those stagnating Lets units to a social services account. The logic being: 'If you don't need to spend those Lets units, we'll give them to someone who needs them more than you do.'

Though the idea would have to be approved by the members it involves some degree of compulsion and nannying. It would mean administrators deciding what is going to happen to individuals' accounts and many members would feel they have lost independence and freedom of choice.

Despite its superficial attractions, this idea may create more problems than it solves. And it certainly prevents members from saving up for a big purchase or a rainy day.

CHAPTER 13

Lets in practice

*One person's bargain is
another's raw deal.*
RICHARD ADAMS

A city system

Bob Merrall and a young woman sit across from each other in the
front room of a terraced house in Withington, south Manchester.

Bob is a man in his sixties: born and bred in the world of business and practical skills. Hair going grey, smartly dressed, his
knowledge of mechanics, electrics, tiling and decorating is extensive. Despite his skills, he is winding up a small business which
has kept him for many years, but which he now views as uneco-
nomic.

His fellow member, on the other hand, is many years younger,
is unemployed and has little money.

Both are people unlikely to meet in the fragmented communities of south Manchester. They clearly move in different circles,
with different interests and different friends.

Indeed their differences are typical of members of Lets, and
without becoming members they might never have met. If money
changed hands between them, it might only be because the
woman saw an advertisement for something Bob was selling.

Their experiences in Lets are also typical — although both are
at different ends of the trading spectrum.

Bob has been in considerable demand for his skills at tiling. 'I
joined Lets because it is a cracking idea,' he said. 'I've always
been good at floor and wall tiling and I'm also a qualified electrician and can offer small domestic electrical alterations.' He is

There is heavy demand for Bob Merrall's tiling on Manchester Lets.
Photo: Linda Boyles

also a skilled mechanic, and although he will give mechanical advice on Lets, he doesn't advertise mechanical services.

'The tiling has gone potty,' he says, 'and I've earned 150 Bobbins tiling a floor and doing a complete kitchen over three days. I've done three electrical jobs. I base my charges at six Bobbins per hour and give a rough estimate beforehand. No one has haggled.

'I do it because I enjoy helping people and I believe in it, although my main business is my living. I would rather pay Bobbins for vegetables instead of cash for the stuff you get in the shops which is rubbish. My Lets work is expanding and I'm saving up the Bobbins to use when my business closes.'

While Bob has (so far) been mainly a seller on Lets, his fellow member has been mainly a buyer. In a year of membership she says she has done a lot of trading: gas fitting work in her house, repairs to her car, and therapy. 'These have all been essentials,' she said, 'but I wouldn't have had the money for them as I am unemployed. Using Lets means things are accessible that weren't before. I am conscious of having a big Lets debt but I don't know how much. I think I deserve some Bobbins for thinking up creative ways of earning them!'

Jo Bend is a member who has also found the system invaluable. She manages to keep her Lets income and spending fairly well balanced. Her home-made bread sells out most weeks, and she uses the Bobbins she earns to pay for car repairs, or lifts home from parts of the city she doesn't feel comfortable travelling through late at night.

Jo's partner tells of a fellow member who is a skilled mechanic but cannot find a job as he has no formal qualifications. 'He jacked in his exams, he looks scruffy, he finds it difficult to put himself across well, and he has no money. But he has real talent and does mechanical jobs on cars in the street. So he earned some Bobbins and bought some letterheadings and cards produced by a member. It has given him a step forward towards self employment as he has been able to distribute them around people and to garages. So now he gets a bit more work and just a little bit of Lets trading is getting him out of a rut.'

These are just some of the people who have flocked to Manchester Lets, making it the country's fastest growing system.

Within eighteen months the group has expanded to 300 members, although Siobhan Harpur, one of the core administrators, believes they are 'just scratching the surface of its potential'. She says, 'It has been amazingly successful in its short lifespan in terms of the growth of membership, the members increasing their trading, and with an annual renewal rate which saw only a few people drop out.

'That must be good evidence that we are providing something that people want.'

The administrators of Manchester Lets are convinced that being efficient has contributed greatly to their success. Co-founder Andy Rickford said: 'We were very thorough when we set up. Three of us got together in July 1992 and we said we would have the system operating by the end of the year. We soon had a core group of eight committed people. We wanted to be clear about what we were each doing and we put a lot of thought and planning into it. We developed an ethos of saying what we were going to do, and doing it.'

Unlike most launches, Manchester Lets had everything in place by the evening of the first public meeting: even the first

The job done — a Lets cheque for 30 Bobbins is made out to Bob Merrall. *Photo: Linda Boyles*

directory was published, and more people were invited to sign up.

Most of the contacts came through word of mouth as the message of this new community activity spread through Manchester. 'We had a lot of media coverage,' said Andy, 'but we tried to avoid it! We expanded because of the quality of our information and our fast and friendly response to people's inquiries.'

The group also organises regular trading fairs which are 'full of bustle and which have been a good source of new members,' says Andy. 'People can come along and see a lot of things happening. They can see the number and range of skills on offer, on the spot and in the Lets directory. They can talk to experienced Lets members to find out how it works in practice. Membership just exploded.'

According to Siobhan, most of the initial activity has been among people who are 'adventurous and risk takers. They may come from different sections of society but it takes a while for those willing to try an innovation to become involved before others join in. People are becoming more adventurous as they gain more confidence in the system. Manchester Lets has created quite a large network of people who otherwise might not have had the opportunity to meet. A lot of people say their lives have improved significantly.'

Manchester has achieved its success against a background of different views of what a Bobbin is worth. According to Siobhan, the Bobbin has a nominal equivalence to the pound, while her daughter Cara values the Bobbin at a lot less. At a tea party for Lets members in Withington, there were several different views as to its value.

For Peter Gay (who offers umbrella repairs amongst other skills) the value of the Bobbin is far less important than the value of the personal relationships that result from the trading. He trades with the informal Bob-A-Jobbers — a small group of members seeking to charge a standard one Bobbin for each job, no matter how big or small.

This group trades within the Manchester system and their aim is to foster community contact between people. When charging a Bobbin for a job to a Lets member who is not a Bob-A-Jobber, they ask that the member charge a single Bobbin for their next job.

Thus they hope more people will trade on the same basis. But Peter Gay admits that when his account balance is published for all members to see, he has uncomfortable feelings because the high minus figure doesn't reflect the actual work he has done on the system.

The Malvern experience

In Malvern Lets members can eat, have their garden dug, buy clothes, find a babysitter, go on holiday, have haircuts, and even get the ironing done. Many of the trades are in mundane everyday items and the range of goods and services on offer are a fair reflection of those found in Lets schemes throughout the country.

George Glide and Pam Allan sell sacks of potatoes, onions, carrots and cabbages for Beacons.

Martin Southam will fix your car or van, and Mollie Nightingale-Smith will do knitting and crochet.

Bric-a-brac and junk is available from Phil Howard's shop, odd jobs can be done by David Hope, and labouring can be hired from Trevor Trueman who likes a change from his usual work as the local GP. The vegetables are in demand, as are the horse-riding lessons offered by Sue Humphreys. A caravan for rent has not yet found a hirer, although a member starting a desktop publishing business has earned some Beacons.

Malcolm Victory will provide architectural plans, and Malvern is the place where the first house has been built for Lets — George and Pam's farm now boasts a handsome tree-house built by John Barton whose more usual line of work is tree cutting and maintenance.

David Wardle who is one of the group's computer experts has earned Beacons from sorting out members' programs. He's spent them on having a tree cut down — which would have cost him pounds if the system had not formed.

Another member paid Martin Southam to attach a towbar to a van, and the trailer he subsequently bought has been hired out.

There are over 60 members one year after the group was founded and the majority have done some trading. The system has organised several 'Tea and Trading' days where members can come together, gossip over cups of tea, and trade with each other.

Such days were particularly useful in the early months when people were getting to know one another, for even though Malvern is a small town, Lets Barter brought together many people who had not previously met.

These are small beginnings perhaps, but the group is slowly expanding. Members are realising they really can spend Beacons before they've earned them, and that they won't be charged interest. Nearly everyone has made some new contacts in the area, and all have learnt something about money and how to use it.

FACTS AND FIGURES

In late 1993 LetsLink UK carried out a survey of the 200 UK Lets groups. 57 systems replied, with the following results. Where averages are shown, it should be remembered that *the figures vary widely* between different systems. It's also likely that the figures for the amount of trading are underestimates, since some members are slow at sending cheques to administrators.

- The highest number of members was 333 and the average membership was 70.
- The average recruitment rate is four people per month.
- Groups double their size in a year until they reach a membership of 250 when the increase slows down.
- Nearly a third of systems don't use computers to maintain the accounts.
- 55 per cent of members are employed or self-employed.
- 12 per cent work part-time.
- 25 per cent are unemployed.
- 2.5 per cent are retired.
- 5 per cent are students or in other categories.
- Over a third of systems had businesses as members.
- Less than 10 per cent of systems had experienced some sort of trading with members in another system.
- 35 per cent of systems do not tie their Lets unit to the pound.
- Each system traded an average of 5200 Lets units per year, though this figure varied widely.
- The highest turnover on an individual account was 7000

units since founding, again with wide variations.
- Members turning over a high number of Lets units are not necessarily in larger systems.
- The youngest member is eight years old and the oldest 90.
- These statistics indicate that the total turnover in Lets in the UK to date may be close to 1.5 million units.

Islets

Islets was designed as the UK's first *national* Lets. Still in embryo form, it was set up following a development weekend of Lets activists in Telford. The participants realised they needed a way of helping Lets members travelling around the country to find accommodation, and to fund Lets meetings.

Islets is based at Telford Lets and the units are called 'Echos' which are equivalent to the pound. Anyone undertaking Lets development work is able to register, but the participants have still to develop the basic framework of how Islets will work and what its main purpose will be. No directory has been produced, and there are still many ideas about how Islets should develop — in particular whether it should expand beyond Lets development work to become a 'normal' system, albeit covering the entire country or world. One possibility is that it become a sort of accommodation exchange allowing people to find a bed for overnight stays while travelling to promote Lets — particularly valuable for members who are frequently asked to give start-up talks.

The Permaculture Exchange

The Permaculture Exchange is the first worldwide system. It is open only to those who have studied permaculture or are members of permaculture associations. (Permaculture is a system of designing all aspects of living and working in harmony with nature). The Exchange has over 100 members in the UK, Holland, France, Finland and Spain.

The group call their Lets unit, 'Stars', 'to reflect the unlimited nature of them,' according to the co-ordinator Jane Hera. She stresses that the services available are not just permaculture designs, and she cites house repairs, language tuition and tree surgery as some of the more 'ordinary' services on offer, and boat delivery (by land or sea) as a more unusual service available. Over 4000 Stars have been traded since it was started in July 1992.

The Exchange publishes its directory twice a year and Jane says it has allowed members to use professional services they would otherwise not have been able to afford. It has also given some formal recognition for work which was previously only voluntary, such as arranging the Permaculture Association's annual 'convergence' which members can now pay to attend partly in Stars.

MultiBarter

MultiBarter, or the National Credit Trading Club, is an idea of David Stephens. He is developing the concept as a way of allowing Lets-type trading over distances. He proposes a directory in several sections, divided according to whether the goods and services are likely to be traded locally, regionally or nationally.

Accounts would be maintained at one national office and members would be issued with cheques or credit transfer slips.

To pump-prime the system he is also proposing that members undertake community work and are credited in Lets which are created from a 'Good Works Account'. This account, he says, would usually run in minus, but its debit would always be limited to 10 per cent of the turnover of the system.

Lets in Australia

Lets has been enthusiastically embraced in Australia and there are nearly 200 systems operating throughout the country. The total membership is believed to be in excess of 30,000 and the largest, in the Blue Mountains, has 1000 accounts encompassing over 2000 people.

The Blue Mountain system operates in an area of 70,000 people where conventional work opportunities either involve commuting to Sydney, or part-time 'multiple jobs'. The Lets network has attracted nearly 50 businesses and the administrators point to an expansion of jobs, and to benefits for businesses which sell in part dollars and part 'Ecos'.

Lets is also beginning to be accepted by the national government for its benefits to the economy: after a campaign the systems are officially accepted as entitled to the Australian equivalent of charitable status, and social security benefits are not affected by Lets earnings.

Local money in history

Although Lets is a new invention, local money issued by individuals and bodies other than national governments has been popular until recent years. Many of these local money systems have been long forgotten, but some were highly successful in their time at facilitating trading between people who had confidence in the local money, but not the national currency.

- In Samoa, handmade woven mats and a form of bark cloth constituted a popular form of money and — like Lets — could be created by people themselves. Across Polynesia and Micronesia, whales' teeth, stones, beads, pigs and feathers were all used as a medium of exchange.

- Nearer home, Liverpool Corporation issued its own notes in response to a financial panic in 1793 caused by the declaration of war by France.

  The Corporation appealed to the Bank of England for £100,000 on the grounds that 'there was an apprehension of a general calamity to the merchants, traders, and inhabitants of this place from the shock to public confidence and from the want of immediate pecuniary resource.'

  The Bank of England, no doubt wary of applications from every city in the land, refused to grant the loan; and the Corporation successfully petitioned parliament for permission to issue its own notes up to the value of its assets. The move was apparently so successful that the notes passed into general circulation, and when the time for redemption came (the Corporation backing the notes) they were able to pay them off early and they asked for the period of the Act to be extended.

- In Gosaba, India, in 1903, one Sir Daniel Hamilton issued his own notes called 'Hachitta' which were paid to people for

153

work done reclaiming land at the mouth of the river Ganges. The notes could be spent at a store Sir Daniel set up. The official backing for the notes was a deposit of 1100 rupees supposedly held at the estate office.

The wording on the notes read: 'Sir Daniel Mackinnon Hamilton promises to pay the bearer on demand, at the Co-operative Bhundar, in exchange for value received, one rupee's worth of rice, cloth, oil or other goods. The value received in exchange for this note may be given in the form of bunds constructed, or tanks excavated, or land reclaimed, or buildings erected, or in medical or educational services. The note may be exchanged for coin, if necessary, at the estate office. The note is made good not by the coin, which makes nothing, but by the assets created and the services rendered. The note is based upon the living man, not on the dead coin. It costs practically nothing, and yields a dividend of 100 per cent in land reclaimed, tanks excavated, and houses built etc. And in a more healthy and abundant life.'

The notes were so successful that in 30 years a large area was drained and turned into highly productive agricultural land supporting over 12,000 people.

■ The year 1932 saw a radical experiment in issuing local money in the town of Wörgl in Austria. There the mayor issued 5000 'free schillings' backed by the same amount of national Austrian schillings. The local council used the free schillings to pay for improvements to public services, and the mayor persuaded local traders to accept the notes as real money. A novel initiative was to charge a fee of 1 per cent a month on the notes. This had to be paid by the person holding the note at the time by buying a stamp to be stuck on the back. If the stamps were not bought, the note became invalid.

The result of this arrangement was that people receiving free schillings spent them as soon as they could to avoid the small 1 per cent fee. Within a year the 5000 free schillings had circulated an estimated 463 times, thus allowing the creation of goods and services valued at over 2,300,000 schillings. The ordinary national schilling only circulated 213 times in the same period.

During the year of operation, Wörgl reduced its unemployment rate by 25 per cent. However, despite its success, the experiment went no further, for despite 300 other towns in Austria preparing to adopt the idea, the Austrian National Bank stepped in to persuade the government to make it illegal to issue such notes.

- During the seventeenth century, clippers crossing the Atlantic faced many difficulties, and the governors of colonies in the New World could not always count on funds arriving in time to pay the garrison troops.

  In 1685 the 'Intendant' of Canada became weary of waiting for the ship to come in from France with the money to pay his troops. In response he requisitioned the troops' playing cards, wrote a value on them, and added his signature. He then declared they could be redeemed when the next shipment of money came in.

  Despite objections from the Bank of France, the traders in the colony agreed to accept the playing card notes which continued in circulation until 1749.

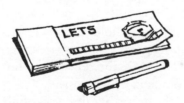

CHAPTER 14

A look in the crystal ball

*So simple, yet so revolutionary,
it's bound to sweep the country.*
THE MAIL ON SUNDAY

One Lets member in the south of England has a not very impressive income of £3000 a year. But during her four-year membership of the local system she has increased this by the equivalent of another £2000 a year in Lets units.

All that income is a boost to the economy of her town: all of it has been earned locally and all of it has been spent locally.

Lets has an almost incredible potential for regenerating local economies and helping people increase their economic activity as well as for helping to restore the sense of community and friendship that much of our society has lost.

But will Lets be able to realise that potential? Will it be able to break out of the world of the chattering classes to be embraced by all as a positive contribution to our lives? Or will short-sighted politicians jump to protect the integrity of sterling, and attempt to make Lets-type transactions unlawful, or at least very difficult?

MultiLETS

We have seen how the Lets idea is being seized upon throughout the UK and abroad, and developed and adapted. The multiple registers idea, examined in Chapter 12, is already coming to pass. Such registries are likely to speed up the formation of new systems, particularly in areas where people feel intimidated by the work of keeping the accounts. They will help link the members of different networks across a region, so although their first attachment may be to the fellow Lets participants in the same district, they will now be able to trade with members of other systems further afield.

Public funding

At the same time as these systems are being developed, local governments are starting to examine how Lets can help the economy. Some farsighted economic development officers have already seen a little of the potential, although national governments are still in the dark ages as far as Lets is concerned. At the time of writing some local councils have agreed to pump-prime Lets development, and while council money is not essential to start a system, it is possible that grant funding may mean the founders can spend more time recruiting members, so increasing the size of systems faster.

As Lets grows across the country, it is possible that in a few short years we will see dramatic changes to the economy.

Different systems for different communities

People are likely in the future to belong to several different systems. They might belong to one where they live and another where they work. They might join another set up by their church, mosque, synagogue or temple. The school their children attend may run one, and if in business, they might be members of a Lets formed by the Chamber of Commerce or the Federation of Small Businesses.

The systems themselves are likely to vary in type. Some will match their credit units to sterling and many transactions will be in a mix of Lets and pounds. Others will cost work hours equally, so people receive the same number of Lets no matter what job they do.

Other schemes may not use Lets credits at all: people will offer services without any record kept of the transactions, and members won't care whether individuals are buying more than they are selling — or vice versa.

Some Lets schemes may be used to measure work done by individuals when projects are first set up and there isn't conventional money available yet to pay the participants. The Lets measure will allow an equal payout when money does become available.

Lets and the mainstream economy

We are living in a world economy where businesses are always trying to increase output per worker, and where the number of people in formal employment is likely to decrease. At the same time the banks teeter on the edge of a debt crisis, and the environment is being seriously damaged by pollution and resource extraction.

All this adds up to an impending crisis for the world of national currencies. For many people, Lets is likely to be seen as the only substitute outside the influence of multinational companies and soul destroying production lines.

As confidence grows, Lets is likely to snowball. As more and more people join, increasing numbers of small businesses will offer goods and services on Lets because they fear customers with sterling to spend simply won't be enough to keep them afloat. More and more businesses as members will mean more of the necessities of life will become available for Lets. Goods sold on Lets which have been made for local consumption are likely to be better produced than those bought from companies whose production centres are many miles away.

At the same time an increasing range of labour-intensive services will be offered. People will be able to have consumer durables repaired more easily because they can pay in Lets whereas the often shoddy replacements from huge companies have to be bought with scarce sterling.

Goods repaired locally will mean fewer lorries delivering to the hyperstore and may relieve pressure on urban streets and the open countryside. Throwing out fewer consumer durables will relieve pressure on landfill sites, reduce pollution, and even reduce council taxes.

These extra jobs, some part-time and many of them flexible enough to fit around the family or unpaid community activities, will mean more people feeling they have a meaningful role in life. More people able to earn in Lets may mean fewer disaffected

youths hanging around on street corners. It could mean more
youth workers running clubs for Lets, and more young people
having somewhere enjoyable to go. As they get to know more
people in their communities, so they are less likely to commit
petty crime. Employing young people for Lets on environmental
projects can reduce vandalism.

Middle aged people made redundant, whether from an office
or a factory, may gain a new lease of life selling their skills for Lets
units. A person accustomed to working who is able to be useful
to fellow members of the community may suffer less stress and
become healthier. In turn, healthier people mean lower costs for
the National Health Service.

Those in full-time work will be able to try other possibilities as they offer services on Lets. As these services attract more and more demand, they may feel confident to leave an uninspiring job which consumes too much of their time. As a result they may become more contented and their families may see more of them.

According to Dr Michael Argyle, the author of *The Psychology of Happiness*, people gain happiness from 'satisfying work, satisfying leisure, a strongly supportive social network, and being extrovert and positive.' Lets addresses all of these.

Schools with insufficient income to pay teachers could employ additional help for Lets units. The children would be given extra attention, and learning would improve so they come out of school more fitted to tackle the complex society they will live in. Giving children more attention and more encouragement will also give them more hope and confidence, and make them less likely to find their way into a spiral of crime and lack of care about people around them. The opportunity for children to do limited buying and selling on Lets will help them to interact with others and be more confident in themselves.

Elderly people in a Lets scheme will feel less need to rely on charity. As their skills are bought on Lets they are less likely to feel they are a burden on society. They will be able to exchange goods and services with younger people, bringing them closer together.

Small businesses are likely to run several different Lets accounts for different systems they belong to. They will be able to climb out of the cycle of debt and high interest charges as many will be able to set up or expand using Lets credits rather than crushing bank loans. They will be encouraged to buy from local suppliers whenever possible because by doing so in Lets they are freed from cashflow difficulties. They will also know that most of the credits they create will remain in the district and are likely to return to their business in the future.

Big businesses will need to look to their laurels. As workers see other opportunities opening before them, they are less likely to settle for poorly paid jobs with bad working conditions in the local fast food joint or sweatshop. Businesses are likely to have to improve their conditions and pay in order to attract workers. In turn, businesses not in Lets will not gain access to the customers their competitors are able to sell to.

This will give a welcome edge to the small businesses in Lets. Large businesses will respond by either ignoring Lets and restricting their trade to sterling, or realising that by buying in from local suppliers, they can spend the Lets they earn.

Lets and government

Governments should perceive these benefits and give Lets every encouragement. They should allow taxes due on Lets earnings to be paid in Lets. This doesn't mean the Inland Revenue only spending the Lets credits on having its offices repainted or its windows cleaned. It means the government can pay councils some of their rate support grant in Lets. It can give grants to businesses in Lets. It can invest in the railways in Lets and even some portion of social security benefits could paid in Lets.

The Treasury would also benefit from a dramatic expansion of Lets. For as Lets encourages local production and a reduction in pollution, so the demands on the public purse will be reduced. At its simplest, fewer lorries transporting goods over long distances may reduce the need for the phenomenally expensive roads programme. Fewer dissatisfied people who can't find work will mean lower unemployment benefit costs, and possible reductions in the budgets of the police and courts.

The real economy

In short, an expansion of Lets will result in increases in the trading most beneficial to ordinary people and least damaging to the environment. It means an expansion in the real economy.

It may also mean some parts of the economy contract. The large impersonal companies which make shoddy goods will face stiffer competition, and the resulting reduced profit margins may leave them with less capital to asset strip other companies, buy up competitors and introduce new technologies just to reduce the workforce.

161

Lets and the Third World

Governments in the Third World and Eastern Europe will be able to benefit from Lets as it can be an effective development tool. Similarly agencies working in undeveloped countries can introduce it as a way to strengthen local economies. Systems could be started to create communities of buyers and sellers across national boundaries. For instance, the growing world of ethical trading could use Lets to bypass international currency markets and transnational loans. All this is still in the future, and there has been very little work on how Lets can be used to reduce the North/South divide, but the possibilities are there, and in time we may see Third World economies rejuvenated using Lets which does not require input from bodies such as the World Bank.

Because Lets builds up trust between people, it also has the potential to reduce tensions in the world's trouble spots. Systems spanning different groups of people can encourage social contacts through trading, leading to a dampening of antagonism and conflict. It can be used in places where ethnic and religious disputes are simmering over a long period. An effective Lets scheme can counteract the influence of inflammatory politicians attempting to whip up hatred. In refugee camps Lets can help people on the road to rebuild their lives by using their skills and knowledge.

Through Lets we will get to know more of the people we see on the high street. More of us will feel we belong in our towns and cities. We will feel less afraid of the local youths because we're more likely to know them.

Fewer of us will fear unemployment because we'll know there are other economic opportunities open to us. We may see fewer people turn to crime as the only way they can respond to formal unemployment.

And more of us will gain contentment as our lives become happier and richer.

APPENDIX I
Inspiration list

A list of goods and services offered and wanted in Lets directories around the country.

Animals
Cat/dog boarding
Animal exercising
Farm sitting
Horse care sharing
Horse and cart for outings
Milking
Veterinary care
Grooming

Arts and crafts
Artists model available
Mural painting, drawing, design
A painting or watercolour of your house
Photo portraits
Illustrations
Design of logos, letterheads, posters
Stained glass
Pottery
Wooden toys
Furniture restoration
Upholstery
Garment making/repairs
Theatre clothes and props
Mounting of photos and cards
Curtain making
Silver jewellery

Leather work/repairs
Candle making
Basketry
Piano tuning/repairs
Sewing machine
Woodwork shop
Jigsaw/drill
Darkroom
Kiln
Silkscreen printing equipment

Building and allied trades
Architectural drawings for extensions/new buildings
Carpentry, joinery and fitted furniture
Machining of wood for DIY
Electrician, small repairs to fires, toasters, lamps etc by retired electrical engineer
Electrician, emergency call out
Wind powered electrical systems installed
Plastering
Sash window repairs
Barrowing, lugging, digging; 'sledge or lump, I won't grump'
Central heating installation
Flooring
Roofing
Pointing
Builder's mate — big, bright & strong

163

Dry stone walling
Interior design
Painting/decorating
Plumbing
Angle grinder
Cement mixer
20ft extending ladder
Mig welder
Natural paints/wood finishes

Business

Accountancy, book-keeping, VAT
Advertising & marketing
Business management
Computer consultancy/programming
Desktop publishing
Ghost writing
Help in business or shop
Office organisation
Help with mailing/distribution
Printing of business cards etc
Proof reading
Typing/editing/word processing
Writing C.V.s, reports etc
Video work
Advice on grant applications, C.V.s
Translations of various languages
Shares in a business project
Wordprocessor
Typewriter
Time on quality computer

Domestic and family

Energy surveys/advice on low energy heating/insulation
Draught excluder installations
Cleaning
Catering for parties
Ironing/washing clothes/collect & deliver

Help with house moving, shifting, packing, cleaning, minding
Weekend childcare
Outings with kids to sea, swimming pools
Wood chopping
Recycling (no more than an estate car load)
China repairs
Video, TV and audio repairs
Handyman — light repairs around the house
Springclean/party clean up
Organising children's parties
Shopping/delivery
House/pet/plant sitting
Babysitting/picking up kids from school
Storytelling to sick children
Oven cleaning
Waiting in for gas/electric people
Dog walking
Folk music performance
"Cocktail pianist"
Puppet theatre/clown
Disc jockey & kit for rent
General maintenance
Kitchen/function room/dining room
Beer/wine making equipment

Food

Jam/winemaking
Cake baking/fruit pies
Jam making from your fruit
Local honey
Fruit — apples/plums in season
Fruit picking
Harvesting
Seasonal organically grown veg
Goats milk
Cooking for special evenings

Oriental meals
Fresh or frozen quiches
Special cakes

Entertainment and leisure

Song writing/ballad singing with
    acoustic guitar
Children's theatre play
Juggler/stilt walker
P.A. system
Marquee for hire

Gardening and landcare

Gardening
Permaculture design workshop
Harvesting
Landscaping
Tree surgery and pruning
Compost making
Log splitting
Gardening tools
Firewood
Part of garden for organic
    allotment
Hive minding and swarm
    catching
Tree planting
Manure and compost
Shredding equipment (large
    scale)
Seeds, bulbs and seedlings
Garden & barbeque for parties

Health and personal

Acupuncture
Alexander Technique
Birth tubs and counselling
Drama therapy
Hands on healing
Massage
Movement and dance therapy
Reflexology
Yoga
Meditation

Physiotherapy
Shiatsu
Addiction counselling
Aromatherapy
Dietary advice
Float sessions
Homeopathy
Co-counselling
A listening ear
Gestalt dream interpretation
Handreading
I-ching and tarot reading
Assertiveness training
Counselling
Care of the elderly
Personal development
Relaxation and stress
    management
Hair dressing
Love letter/poetry writing

**Property and
accommodation**

House sitting
Dry storage space for hire
Function room & kitchen for
    hire
Bed & Breakfast (for your friends
    when you haven't got space)
Caravan for short holidays
Tipi to hire
Rooms, studios, barns to share

Transport

Car share
Drive your car to the airport
Taxi service
Small van deliveries/removals
Lifts to and from work
Car/van/lorry hire
Lifts to the seaside, moors,
    picnics
Trailer hire
Car repairs

165

Bicycle repairs
Car welding
Car cleaning
Installation of stereos
Motorcycle restoration
Vehicle for sale

Tuition/education
Personal tuition
Piano, saxophone, etc lessons
Song and song writing
Painting/drawing
Swimming, snorkelling, diving

Cooking
Language
Computers, DTP
Weaving/spinning lessons
Special needs
Music sessions
Dance
Sewing/dressmaking
Horse riding
DIY
Darkroom photography
Chess

APPENDIX 2
Members' agreements

1   The LetsLink model

1   The Local Exchange Trading System is a non-profit membership society or club whose rights and authority are vested in the members who delegate that authority to the management group/core group/steering group (delete as applicable) who act on their behalf.

2   The Lets system provides an information service through which members can exchange goods and services, and maintains a central account of those exchanges for the benefit of members.

3   Members agree to the Lets system holding their details on computer and distributing to other members those details relevant to the purpose of exchange. Members also agree to the directory of goods and services being distributed to the general public for publicity purposes.

4   Members may give or receive from each other credit in the accepted Lets unit of account called... These units are considered to represent the value of (e.g. one pound, one hour's work) and are recorded centrally on Lets.

5   Only the account holder can authorise the transfer of units from their account to that of another.

6   No money is deposited or issued. Members may engage in any transaction entirely in Lets units, or on a part cash basis, but only Lets units are recorded on the Lets system.

7 All accounts start at zero. Members are not obliged to be in receipt of any credit before issuing another member with credit from their account, subject to any limit that may be set by the management group from time to time.

8 No member is obliged to accept any particular invitation to trade, or to engage in any transaction whatsoever with other members. On leaving the Lets system however, members with commitments outstanding are obliged to balance their account.

9 Any member is entitled to know the balance and turnover of another member's account. The management group may also decide from time to time to publish the balances and turnovers of all accounts.

10 No interest is charged or paid on balances. The management group is authorised to charge joining or renewal fees in Lets units and/or sterling on a cost-of-service basis as the situation requires, and to levy service charges on members' accounts at rates assessed in consultation with the membership or advisory group.

11 The Lets system administrator may decline to record an account or directory entry considered inappropriate for legal or other reasons.

12 No warranty or undertaking as to the value, condition or qualiy of services or items exchanged is expressed or implied by virtue of the introduction of members to each other. The Lets system publishes a list of the resources and services made available by members but cannot be held responsible for the actual goods and services on offer.

13 Members are individually responsible for their own personal tax liabilities and returns. The Lets system has no obligation or liability to report to the tax authorities or to collect taxes on their behalf.

14 Members have the right and are encouraged to attend any meeting of the management group and to participate in decision making. Members have a right of appeal to the advisory group on all management decisions.

15 The management group may act on behalf of members in seeking explanation or satisfaction from a person whose activity is considered to be contrary to the interests of the membership.

The management group, in consultation with the advisory group, may suspend membership in the case of delinquent accounts and in the last resort may remove members from the system.

The management group may also reserve the right to deny membership to an applicant in exceptional circumstances at their discretion.

16 Membership of the Lets system implies acceptance of the conditions of this agreement.

2 **The Landsman definition and account holder agreement**
   (The LETSystem as defined by Landsman Community
   Services Ltd).

   A LETSystem, Local Exchange Trading System, is a self-regulating
   network which allows its users to issue and manage their own
   money supply within the boudaries of the network.

   The LETSystem accounting service maintains a system of accounts
   for its users.

   Essential characteristics

   A LETSystem has the following essential characteristics:

1 A service to the community. Administrative costs are recovered, in
   the internal currency, from each account according to the cost of the
   service. The system operates on a not-for-profit basis.

2 Consent is required at all times. There is never any obligation to
   trade. It is the account holders who have control over the movement of money out of their accounts. The administration can only
   act on the instructions of the account holder who is making the
   payment. All accounts start at zero, no money is deposited or
   issued.

3 Key information is available to all account holders. Any account
   holder may know the balance (the degree of commitment) and
   trading volume (the level of participation) of another account on the
   system.

4 A convenient measure. The unit of account is a measure equivalent
   to the national currency.

5 Your money belongs to you. Your money is personal, in every way
   your own money. No interest is charged or paid on balances.

   A personal money network that adopts all the above criteria and
   agreements is a LETSystem.

   Account holder agreement

1 A LETSystem is based on the free association of individuals (the
   users) who take out accounts on the system. The LETSystem
   Registry provides a service which allows account-holders to
   exchange information to support trading, and maintains such
   accounts of that trading as users request.

   The account holders delegate the maintenance of these accounts to
   the Recording Co-ordinators. The account holders also delegate
   responsibilities to Stewards as stated in this agreement.

2   Account holders shall be willing to consider trading in local currency.

3   TheRecording Co-ordinators will transfer local currency from one user's account to that of another only on the authority of the account-holder making payment.

4   The stewards may instruct the Recording Co-ordinators to decline to record an acknowledgement considered inappropriate.

5   The unit of exchange is a measure equivalent to the pound sterling.

6   An account-holder may know the balance and trading volume of another account-holder.

7a Accountability for taxes incurred by users is the obligation of those involved in an exchange, the LETSystem Registry and its agents including the Recording Co-ordinators and stewards have no obligation nor authority nor liability to report to taxation authorities or to collect taxes on their behalf.

7b No warranty or undertaking as to value, condition, or quality of the items exchanged is expressed or implied by virtue of the introduction of users to each other.

7c Account holders agree to the recording of any information that they supply and to the holding of all such information on computer. While all information, excepting balance and turnover of accounts, is considered personal and confidential, neither the LETSystem Registry nor its agents can guarantee that confidentiality, or necessarily be held liable for any breach of it.

8   The Steward is authorized to levy charges on users' accounts in internal currency at rates assessed by the Steward in liaison with the Recording Co-ordinators and the Advisors.

Signed...

Date...

These agreements are sufficient to define the responsibilities of all parties in a contractual arrangement. There is no need for a constitution which would be against the community and personal ethics of LETSystems.

APPENDIX 3
A model constitution for Lets

This constutution is produced by LetsLink but is still under development.

1 Name

The name of the organisation is ... Lets, referred to as 'the system' in this Constitution.

2 Aims and objectives

2.1 To develop and encourage the experience of Community in ... through the establishment of a local exchange trading system.

2.2 To stimulate the creation of social and economic benefits by and for its members and the people of the locality of .....

3 Membership

3.1 Membership of the system shall be open without prejudice to any individual or organisation sympathetic to the aims of the system, subject to restrictions that may be applied by theManagement Group in exceptional cases, such as for abuse of the system.

3.2 Membership shall be dependent on (a) the payment of membership fees, renewable annually or otherwise at the discretion of the Management Group; and (b) the applicant's endorsement of the ... Lets Members Agreement and Constitution.

4 Legal status

4.1 ...Lets is an unincorporated members' club of people willing to trade amongst themselves.

5 Organisational basis

5.1 The rights and authority of .....Lets are vested in all members, who delegate that authority to a MANAGEMENT GROUP to act on their behalf.

5.1a The Management Group is responsible for ensuring that the tasks of running the system are effectively carried out.

5.1b The Management Group includes all those who have taken on the tasks of running the system, and especially the co-ordinator, accountant, treasurer, directory producer, membership secretary and fundraiser.

5.1c Only members of Lets can join the Management Group.

5.2 An Advisory Group is initiated by the members, or otherwise by the Management Group. Its functions are as follows:

5.2a To oversee and advise the Management Group on the organisation and development of the system as a whole.

5.2b To feedback information and advice on the management, organisation and direction of the system between the members and the Management Group.

5.2c To act as a member liaison and support group, presenting the proposals, opinions, advice and complaints of any members who may be unable to speak directly to the Management Group.

5.2d The Advisory Group is composed of Lets members who are not carrying out the regular tasks of running the system.

5.2e The Group may also include advisors who are not members of the system.

5.2f At least one Advisory Group member will normally attend Management Group meetings.

5.3 An Arbitration Group is set up with the following functions:

5.3a To ensure the accountability of the Management Group to the membership.

5.3b To adjudicate in any cases of dispute between members, or between members and the Management Group.

The group consists of two people, who may also be members of the Advisory Group. They will meet from time to time as necessary.

Management Group meetings will also normally be attended by one Arbitrator.

5.4 The first committee of the system shall consist of the initiating group members. They will arrange and publicise to all members a first AGM within 12 months of their first meeting.

6 Decision-making process

6.1 Every member is entitled to one vote at general meetings.

6.2 The members at the AGM shall appoint a Management Group, an Advisory Group, and Arbitrators.

6.3 Nominations for membership of the Management, Advisory and Arbitration Groups are invited before the start of the AGM. Any member in good standing is eligible for election at the AGM.

6.4 Consensus vote shall be the preferred means of decision-making. (The exact method of election shall be determined by the first committee for the first AGM, thereafter by the Management Group).

7 Functions of the LETS management group

7.1 The Management Group undertakes the executive management of the system, apportioning such roles and functions as necessary to

171

maintain the system in the interests of the membership as a whole, including:

7.1a Maintaining an up-to-date list of all members.

7.1b Recording accurately members' transactions, and supplying accounts.

7.1c Publishing directories.

7.1d Communicating with the membership and taking note of their opinions.

7.1e Maintaining the financial viability of the system.

8 Management group meetings

8.1 The Management Group shall arrange and determine the timing and frequency of its meetings. This will normally be at least every 3 months, and more frequently at the outset.

8.2 The Group shall publicise its meetings in advance to all members, normally through the regular system mailing or newsletter.

8.3 The Group shall keep a record of all its meetings, and make these available to all members in the regular mailings.

8.4 Group meetings are open for any member to attend and make a contribution.

8.5 The quorum shall be a majority or 4 members of the Group, whichever is larger.

8.6 Any Group member who is absent from 3 consecutive meetings without good reason or notice shall be deemed to have resigned their position, and shall be notified to that effect.

8.7 The Group may co-opt new members onto the Group, given the consent by majority vote of the Group. Members so appointed hold office only until the following AGM, but are eligible for re-election at the meeting. Members may also be appointed for a shorter trial period.

8.8 Any Group member may be dismissed for reasons of exceptional mismanagement or gross misconduct by a three-quarters majority vote of the entire Group.

8.9 At least one member of the Advisory Group and one Arbitrator shall also normally be present and empowered to vote at Group meetings.

9 General meetings

9.1 The Management Group shall organise an Annual General Meeting once in every calendar year.

9.2 The Group shall arrange General Meetings (including Extraordinary General Meetings) either at the request of their own members, or at the request of at least 4 members of the system.

9.3 Fourteen days notice of each General Meeting, or 7 days notice of an Extraordinary General Meeting, shall be given to Members.

9.4 Membership entitles each holder to vote at any General Meeting.

10 Finance

10.1 Any monies received shall be paid into the ... Lets account at the ... branch of the ... bank (or at such other bank as the Management Group shall decide from time to time).

10.2 Any monies received or paid out in the name of the system shall be paid into or from the system account. The Management Group shall decide from time to time which signatories can be accepted for financial transactions with the bank.

10.3 No member shall derive any sterling benefit from the system, other than the payment of reasonable expenses.

10.4 Members can be paid reasonable wages in Lets for administrative work carried out in agreement with the Management Group.

10.5 Any Management Group member who carries out an agreed activity on behalf of the system will not be held personally liable for reasonable debts, and will be entitled to be indemnified from the system funds provided that no payment shall be made, or obligation entered into, which cannot be met from the balances of funds held by the system.

10.6 A copy of the most recent annual statements of accounts (in both the sterling and Lets accounts) shall be made available to any member on request, and shall be presented at each AGM.

10.7 ...Lets is a non-profitmaking organisation. Any surplus funds over and above the running costs and development costs of the system will be directed to the ... Lets Community Fund.

10.8 Decision-making on the uses of the ... Lets Community Fund will be subject to consultation with the members at a meeting, publicised to all members in advance. Members may vote in person or by proxy. Decision-making will be by majority vote, and will include the votes of all the members of the Management, Advisory and Arbitration Groups.

11 Changes to the constitution

11.1 Any changes to this constitution can only be made by a 2/3 majority vote at a General Meeting. At least two thirds of the Management Group and 5 other members shall attend. Notices giving full details of the proposed changes shall be posted to all members at least 14 days before the meeting.

12 Winding up

12.1 The system can only be wound up after a consultation process with all the members. A notice of an Extraordinary General Meeting will be sent to all members at least one month before it is held. The notice will invite all members to a meeting to discuss ways of enabling the system to continue, and inviting members to come forward as candidates for the various management roles.

12.2 The system can only be wound up by a two thirds majority vote at a General Meeting. At least two thirds of the Management Group and 5 other members shall attend. A notice giving full details will have been posted to all members at least 14 days before the meeting.

12.3 After settling all debts and obligations, any remaining property shall be transferred to an organisation with similar aims, to be decided at the meeting.

APPENDIX 4
Organisations and information

LetsLink

LetsLink is the national UK grouping of Lets organisations and individual members which supports new systems and acts as a national voice for Lets.

The organisation comprises the Letslink UK Agency which provides advice, information packs, press cuttings, lists of operating systems, sample directories, application forms, videos, start-up games and other stationery for groups to use. It was set up by Liz Shephard to test out a variety of community-based currency models and it develops best practice guidelines and produces the materials used by most systems in the UK. LetsLink also provides advice and speakers to new and existing systems.

The LetsLink UK Network comprises individuals and systems which share practical experience, ideas, best innovations, and news from around the UK and worldwide.

The Network produces a quarterly newsletter detailing Lets developments in the UK and abroad. An annual Lets Camp is also organised, and occasional conferences, training sessions and workshops.

The work of the LetsLink UK Agency is undertaken in association with a Management Group of members of the Letslink UK Network.

Membership rates are £20 for Lets groups, and £10 for individuals. A starter pack is available for £6.25.

More information is available from LetsLink UK, 61 Woodcock Road, Warminster, Wilts. BA12 9DH. Tel/fax 0985 217871.

Lets Solutions

Lets Solutions is currently developing a project to offer training and education in system practice. It promotes Lets and the benefits to businesses, voluntary organisations, and local authorities. Lets Solutions offers talks, training, seminars, consultancy services for local authorities, and advice on all aspects of starting a system.

More information is available from Lets Solutions, 68 Ashford Road, Withington, Manchester M20 9EH Tel. (061) 434 8712; E Mail: LD-MAN-Harpur@MCR1:Geonet.de.

Landsman Community Services Ltd

Landsman is a company formed by Michael Linton, the original designer of Lets. It is registered in Canada and exists to promote the LETSystem worldwide. Landsman initiates special projects and development work to encourage LETSystems. It records unique LETSystem development work by a system of accounts with participants 'entitled to a share of the proceeds' of the company.

More information from Landsman Community Services Ltd., 1600 Embleton Crescent, Courtenay, BC, Canada V9N 6N8 (tel (604) 338 0213); or from Angus Soutar, 1 Bourne End Farm Cottages, Wootton, Bedford, MK43 9AP. Tel 0234 768272.

The Landsman *Design Manual for LETSystems* is available from Worldly Goods, 10-12 Picton Street, Montpelier, Bristol BS6 5QA. Tel 0272 420165.

Further information

Computer registration

Data Protection Registrar, Wycliffe House, Watter Lane, Wilmslow, Cheshire SK9 5AF. The Registrar operate a helpline on 0625 535777.

Computer programmes

Richard Knights, 31D High Street, Totnes, Devon TQ9 5PH.
David Wardle, 4 Merick Road, Malvern Link, Worcs. WR14 1DD

Constitutions

Keith Mitchell, The Thrupp, Thrupp Lane, Thrupp, Stroud, Glos. GL5 2ER

National Council for Voluntary Organisations, Regents Wharf, 8 All Saints Street, London N1 9RL. Tel. 071-713 6161

100 clubs

The Gaming Board for Great Britain, Berkshire House, 168-173 High Holborn, London WC1V 7AA. Tel. 071-240 0821.

Further reading

Bringing the Economy Home from the Market by Ross Dobson. Published in Canada by Black Rose Books and available in the UK from Jon Carpenter Publishing, PO Box 129, Oxford OX1 4PH. Price £12.99 post free.

After the Crash by Guy Dauncey. Second edition published by Green Print, 10 Malden Road, London NW5 3HR.

Index